ON

DE BEAUVOIR

Sally J. Scholz
Villanova University

 **Wadsworth**
Thomson Learning™

Australia • Canada • Denmark • Japan • Mexico • New Zealand • Philippines
Puerto Rico • Singapore • Spain • United Kingdom • United States

Printed in the United States of America
1 2 3 4 5 6 7 03 02 01 00 99

For permission to use material from this text, contact us:
Web: www.thomsonrights.com
Fax: 1-800-730-2215
Phone: 1-800-730-2214

For more information, contact:
Wadsworth/Thomson Learning
10 Davis Drive
Belmont, CA 94002-3098
USA
www.wadsworth.com

ISBN: 0-534-57603-6

Acknowledgments

Special thanks to Thomas Busch, Christopher Kilby, Daniel Kolak, and Shannon Mussett for reading and commenting on the manuscript. Their comments were invaluable to me. William McBride continues to be an important mentor and friend. I especially want to thank Christopher Kilby and Tessa Scholz Kilby for their constant support and assistance.

Table of Contents

Chapter 1   Existentialist Feminist 1
Chapter 2   Biography 6
Chapter 3   Ontology and the "Other" 19
Chapter 4   Existentialist Ethics 30
Chapter 5   Oppression of Women 45
Chapter 6   Liberation 82

Bibliography 86

1

Existentialist Feminist

1999 marks the 50th anniversary of the publication of *The Second Sex*, a book that radically changed how women understand themselves, their relationships, and the social expectations of their gender. Even 50 years after its publication, *The Second Sex* remains unmatched in its scope and depth of analysis. No other book has so profoundly influenced the situation and status of women all over the world. This monumental work on women, grounded in existentialism, is the work of Simone de Beauvoir.

Simone de Beauvoir (1908-1986) helped to popularize the existentialist movement through her novels, essays, and philosophical treatises. *The Second Sex* is undoubtedly her most famous book, but it is by no means her only. Indeed, she was a prolific writer as well as an ardent activist. Beauvoir chose literature as her favored means of expression but her novels are replete with philosophical ideas. She claimed that Jean-Paul Sartre was her primary philosophical influence. Sartre and Beauvoir met as students preparing for the agrégation and maintained an intimate intellectual relationship until Sartre's death in 1980. The philosophical influence was mutual and their impact on existentialism profound. Beauvoir's philosophy was also highly influenced by G.W.F. Hegel, Edmund Husserl, Karl Marx, Friedrich Engels, Sigmund Freud, and Jean-Jacques Rousseau. From Hegel, she took the dialectic as method and the master/slave confrontation as model for the self/other confrontation. Husserl lent the phenomenological method, a form of descriptive analysis. From Marx and Engels, she borrowed a dialectical materialist analysis of history and an optimistic expectation for socialism. Freud and other psychoanalysts offered a

1

conception of the individual as body which Beauvoir turned into embodied consciousness rejecting Freudian determinism. Finally, from Rousseau, Beauvoir gained an appreciation of childhood social influences on individual freedom. Given all these influences, existentialism remains the most important. The rest of this chapter briefly presents some of the central concepts of Beauvoir's existentialism before turning to feminism.

Gaining prominence in the 20th century, existentialism has its roots much earlier in the work of Hegel, Kierkegaard, and Nietzsche among others. It is a movement that in some way defies definition. More than a philosophy, existentialism describes an attitude toward life. The various thinkers categorized as existentialists disagree on such profound philosophical "truths" as the existence of God and the meaning of death. In spite of these differences, they gained the title "existentialist" for their focus on the individual and the individual's role in providing meaning to life. Existentialism denies the validity of ready made systems; systems imply an external source of meaning or a given set of values. On the contrary, existentialism charges the individual with the responsibility of choosing a set of values through his or her actions. In other words, a person's destiny is his or her own making.

In Beauvoir's brand of existentialism, God and rationalism, among other totalizing notions, are rejected in favor of the individual's freedom. Notable in this regard is the rejection of any sort of human nature. Accepting a notion of human nature implies an acceptance of a metaphysical system. The existentialist critique of traditional metaphysics emphasizes the limiting function of concepts of human nature on human freedom. If one's nature is determined, then one's power to choose, to create one's own destiny or meaning each moment, is ineffective.

Beauvoir, like many of her contemporaries, replaces human nature with a universal human condition. Ultimately, the most important feature of that condition is freedom, or as Beauvoir says, freedom as ambiguity. An ambiguous existence is an existence the meaning of which "must be constantly won" (1948, 129). This differs from an absurd existence in that the latter is a meaningless existence. While existentialism is often negatively cast as presenting existence as absurd, Beauvoir's optimistic existentialism, with its attempt at formulating an ethics, requires meaning to be not only possible but necessarily arrived at in the midst of others.

This brings us back to the individual as consciousness. If the individual is responsible for winning his or her own meaning then that individual interprets the world, and himself/herself within the world, in a particular way. The being of things is called being-in-itself; the being of consciousness is called being-for-itself. Being aware of oneself as an object in the world as well as a meaning-giving subject, is self-conscious

2

existence. In contrast, occupying one's place in the world without taking responsibility for it is treating the self as object; it is merely *being*. The self is both subject and object (embodied consciousness). Insofar as the individual (or existent) fails to recognize herself or himself as embodied consciousness responsible for the meaning of her or his existence, that individual is in bad faith. Bad faith may also be thought of as self-deception. When I lie to myself, I treat myself as object.

Freedom allows consciousness the ability to imagine alternatives to a situation or effect an attitude in response to a given condition, freedom is a structural condition of human consciousness. The specific situation within which a person acts — what is given — is facticity. In freely acting within a given situation the individual ceases to *be* as object and begins *existing*; the self, then, emerges somewhere between freedom and facticity. But the action in freedom must be directed toward a project. The project is the ultimate choice or life-direction of the individual. It must not, however, be thought of as a static end-point or final goal of one's existence. Instead, the project is chosen in freedom but also embodies freedom itself. That being the case, the project is constantly chosen. Each action or decision the individual undertakes is directed toward this project, dynamically recreating the project as it aims at it.

By way of example, consider Beauvoir herself. She was born to a bourgeois family in the early part of the 20th century. Education was largely determined by one's sex. As a result, Beauvoir's early schooling aimed at preparing her to assume the role of wife and mother. She responded to these aspects of her facticity, in part, by deciding very early that she would be a writer and re-committing herself to that choice throughout her life. Between the givens of her situation and the absolute freedom of the human existential condition, Beauvoir emerged as a unique individual. She offers her own philosophical account of her life project in the last volume of her autobiography, *All Said and Done:*

> Yet there are some very old bonds in my life that have never been broken. Its essential unity is provided by two factors: the place that Sartre has always had in it, and my faithfulness to my original design--that of knowing and of writing. What did I aim at in this project? Like all living individuals, I sought to overtake my being, to rejoin and merge with it; and in order to do so I based myself upon those experiences in which I had the illusion of having achieved this. Knowing meant directing my awareness towards the world, as did the meditation of my childhood, withdrawing the world from the void of the past and from the darkness of absence: when I lost myself in the object upon which I gazed, or in moments of physical or emotional

3

ecstasy, or in the delight of memory, or in the heart-raising anticipation of what was to come, it seemed to me that I brought about the impossible junction between the in-itself and the for-itself. And I also wanted to realize myself in books that, like those I had loved, would be existing objects for others, but objects haunted by a presence — my presence. (1974a, 28-29)

Further examples of responding to one's situation are found in contrasting the situation of oppression with that of liberation. Beauvoir does that in her articulation of woman's situation in *The Second Sex*. There she uses the Hegelian terms transcendence and immanence to describe the individual's freedom. While each person is both immanence and transcendence, oppression may keep some from exercising their transcendence. "Transcendence" describes the ability of the individual to freely pursue a project thereby acting on the world in an important way. "Immanence" is the condition of endless repetition of mundane tasks that do not impact history. For example, housework, which each day must begin anew, is an activity of immanence. Writing, wherein the writer creatively interprets the world for others to read, may be an activity undertaken in transcendence. The key to understanding woman's oppression is that women have been relegated to a sphere of activity that cuts them off from their transcendence.

Simone de Beauvoir is credited with touching off the second wave of feminism with her analysis of the specific conditions of the oppression of women in *The Second Sex*. The first wave of feminism was characterized by a struggle for legal, economic, and political equality. Although the first wave began in the 17th century, its most active period in the 19th and early 20th centuries focused on winning women the right to vote. The second wave of feminism was most active in the 1960s and 1970s. It was characterized by a much deeper analysis of woman's oppression and liberation. Reading *The Second Sex* it is clear why Beauvoir's work sparked this resurgence of feminist activity. Beauvoir opened the door to a wider variety of analyses concerning the oppressive aspects of woman's situation. This inspired more women to question their situation and struggle to attain liberty.

"Feminism," like "existentialism," indicates a vast number of different groups loosely affiliated by their interest in ending the subordination of women. Feminists do not speak with one voice, nor do they offer a unified conception of woman's plight and struggle. The differences among feminists range from the trivial to the profound. For instance, Beauvoir argued for women to create themselves anew in liberty through unexploited work. She argued that marriage and maternity in the

1940s were conditioned by social expectations that inhibited woman's freedom. More recently, some feminists have argued that motherhood demonstrates women's unique characteristics and might be used as a model for moral theory. The nurturing and care entailed in mothering indicate woman's essential nature. In other words, the two positions in this example examine the feminist issue of "motherhood" from decidedly different perspectives. The existential feminism of Beauvoir views motherhood as a socially constructed practice that can only be undertaken in freedom when social conditions for women are transformed. The cultural feminism of the opposing position contends that the virtues of motherhood are a positive part of woman's nature or essence that need no social transformation but only a social revaluing, i.e., society needs to recognize the important work women as mothers perform.

Although some feminists argue that we are now in the midst of the third wave of feminism, characterized by a still deeper analysis into the very conceptual structures and language that order woman's oppression, we cannot overlook the important contributions of Simone de Beauvoir. She began the discussion of gender construction but even more importantly, she was one of this century's greatest thinkers. Her work begins with concrete lived experience. Hers is a literature of commitment, she used her work to awaken the social conscience and question individual responsibility.

This book introduces readers to her life and philosophy. Beauvoir presented many of her philosophical ideas in her novels which makes interpretation somewhat more challenging. I have included an extensive bibliography to assist the interested reader in pursuing primary and secondary material about various aspects of Beauvoir's life and thought. I begin with a brief biography of this intriguing thinker. Perhaps more than any other philosopher, Beauvoir used her own life experiences in her theorizing.

2
Biography

Simone de Beauvoir was born on January 9, 1908 to Françoise Brasseur de Beauvoir and Georges de Beauvoir. Her full name is Simone Ernestine Lucie Marie Bertrand de Beauvoir. Beauvoir explains each aspect of the name: Simone was chic, Ernestine was in honor of her paternal grandfather, Lucie was her maternal grandmother, Marie is in tribute to the virgin Mary, Bertrand was a family name, and the de indicates that they were of some social status. Simone was the oldest of two daughters; Hélène de Beauvoir was born in 1910. Their mother, Françoise, was devoutly Catholic and Simone herself adopted that devotion during her childhood and early adolescence. Georges had a passion for the theater and gave his daughter an appreciation of literature. Beauvoir's family was of the bourgeoisie and rejecting this familial background led her to explore individual freedom in light of childhood conditioning. In particular, she used the experience of her childhood friend, Zaza, as contrasted with her own experience, to illustrate how freedom must be won away from social expectations which destine one to a predetermined role.

Beauvoir met Elizabeth LeCoin, whom she called "Zaza" in her memoirs, while they were both quite young school girls. Zaza was, in a sense, Beauvoir's first love; she was bold and unpredictable where Beauvoir was shy and dutiful. It was through this childhood relationship that Beauvoir began to question her relationship to other consciousnesses — if she was the absolute, the giver of meaning, how could another consciousness exist that might disrupt her representation of the world? And how could she love another without forfeiting her autonomous self?

Beauvoir continued to raise the question of how one consciousness can authentically relate to another throughout her life.

Zaza was from a similar Catholic, bourgeois background but was much more affected by the constrictions of those family values than Beauvoir herself. While still a student, Zaza fell in love with Maurice Merleau-Ponty in spite of the arranged marriage her family had presumed for her. This relationship proved doomed when the LeCoin's discovered the circumstances of Merleau-Ponty's birth. They forbade their daughter to marry him and indeed forbid her to see Beauvoir whom they thought was a corrupting influence on Zaza. Zaza died in 1929 of what is believed to be encephalitis but Beauvoir believed she died because she loved too dearly — her parents and Merleau-Ponty — and suffered a broken heart. She thought Zaza was so conflicted between her duty to her family and her duty to her freedom that she was forced into the only possible solution, death. This experience had a profound impact on Beauvoir and she attempted to relate the story numerous times (1959, 353-382; 1979, 116-166). Ultimately, she thought she had won her own freedom with Zaza's death, that Zaza could not break free from her situation.

Even early on, Beauvoir was interested in her own capacity to act creatively on the world. She was reading at the age of three and writing not long after that. Her sister, whom everyone called "Poupette," served as her student as well as her comrade against their overly protective mother. Beauvoir describes the important role her sister played in her development in *Memoirs of a Dutiful Daughter:*

> Teaching my sister to read, write, and count gave me, from the age of six onward, a sense of pride in my own efficiency. I liked scribbling phrases or pictures on sheets of paper: but then I knew only how to create imitation objects. When I started to change ignorance into knowledge, when I started to impress truths upon a virgin mind, I felt I was at last creating something real. I was not just imitating grown-ups; I was on their level, and my success had nothing to do with their indulgence. It satisfied in me an aspiration that was more than mere vanity. Until then, I had contented myself with responding dutifully to the care that was lavished upon me: but now, for the first time, I, too, was being of service to someone. I was breaking away from the passivity of childhood and entering the great human circle in which everyone is useful to everyone else. Since I had started working seriously time no longer flew by, but left its mark on me: by sharing my knowledge with another, I was fixing time on another's memory, making it doubly secure.

Thanks to my sister I was asserting my right to personal freedom: she was my accomplice, my subject, my creature. It is plain that I only thought of her as being "the same, but different," which is one way of claiming one's pre-eminence. (1959, 48-49)

One way Beauvoir's discovery of freedom manifested itself was through her declaration in adolescence that she no longer believed in God. Already she was developing the ideas that would inform her mature philosophical thought. Her rejection of God was also a recognition of her own power to shape her life. Throughout her memoirs Beauvoir relates her intense feelings at the realization that she was responsible for providing meaning to her life. At times, such as when she was studying arduously to attain her degree, this filled her with pride and even optimism. At other times, as when she realized the certainty of death, it filled her with anguish:

One night,... just as I was lying down to sleep,... I was overwhelmed by a terrible anguish; I had on occasion been terrified by the thought of death, to the point of tears and screams; but this time it was worse: life was already tilting over the brink into absolute nothingness; at that instant I felt a terror so violent that I very nearly went to knock on my mother's door and pretend to be ill, just in order to hear a human voice. Finally I fell asleep, but I retained a horrifying memory of that awful attack of nerves. (1959, 219)

Beauvoir responded to the responsibility for her destiny by identifying literature as her project. She completed the baccalauréat in philosophy and mathematics and began taking courses at the Sorbonne in 1926. There she studied literature and philosophy to become a teacher. This caused no slight source of turmoil for Beauvoir and her family. It was customary among their social class for young women to marry but the Beauvoir family's financial situation would not provide for a proper dowry. In addition, her father viewed teaching as somewhat base so it was with reluctance that he accepted his daughter's chosen profession.

Nonetheless, Beauvoir continued to work quite diligently and completed her certificate of letters in 1927. By 1929 she was prepared to take the philosophy agrégation exam — an exam that would qualify her to teach. The following lengthy passage from *Memoirs of a Dutiful Daughter* is her own description of this time in her life. Notably, she was a student with philosopher Maurice Merleau-Ponty and anthropologist Claude Lévi-Strauss. In addition, this passage reveals how she viewed her status as woman on her life projects.

I went on working furiously; everyday I spent from nine to ten hours at my books. In January I did my student-teaching stint at the Lycee Janson de Sailly.... My fellow student teachers were Merleau-Ponty and Levi-Strauss;....There were foggy mornings when I felt it was ridiculous to discourse upon the life of the emotions to forty boys who obviously couldn't care less about it; but when the weather was fine, I used to take an interest in what I was saying, and I used to think that in certain eyes I could catch glimmers of intelligence. I recalled my former emotions when I used to pass by the College Stanislas: all this had seemed so far away, so inaccessible--being in a classroom full of boys! And now here I was out in front of the class, and it was I who was giving the lessons. I felt that there was nothing in the world I couldn't attain now.

I certainly didn't regret being a woman; on the contrary it afforded me great satisfaction. My upbringing had convinced me of my sex's intellectual inferiority, a fact admitted by many women.... This handicap gave my successes a prestige far in excess of that accorded to successful male students: I felt it was something exceptional even to do as well as they did; in fact, I hadn't met a single male student who seemed at all extraordinary; the future was as wide open to me as it was to them: they had no advantage over me. Nor did they lay claim to any; they treated me without condescension, and even with a special kindness, for they didn't look upon me as a rival; girls were judged in the competition by the same standards as boys, but they were accepted as supernumeraries, and there was no struggle for the first places between the sexes. That is why a lecture I gave on Plato brought me unreserved compliments from my fellow students -- in particular from Jean Hippolyte. I was proud of having won their esteem. Their friendliness prevented me from ever taking up that "challenging" attitude which later was to cause me so much dismay when I encountered it in American women: from the start, men were my comrades, not my enemies. Far from envying them, I felt that my own position, from the very fact that it was an unusual one, was one of privilege...

Yet I did not renounce my femininity... In Montparnasse I had caught glimpses of elegant beauties; but their lives were too different from mine for the comparison to overwhelm me; besides, once I was free, with money in my pocket, there would be nothing to stop me imitating them... I liked to look at myself, just as I was, in mirrors; I liked what I saw. In the things we had in common, I fancied that I was no less ill-equipped than other women and I felt no resentment toward them... In many respects I set Zaza [and] my sister ... above

9

my masculine friends, for they seemed to me more sensitive, more generous, more endowed with imagination, tears, and love. I flattered myself that I combined "a woman's heart and a man's brain." Again I considered myself to be unique — the One and Only. (1959, 313-315)

At age 21, Beauvoir became the youngest person ever in France to pass the agrégation. She was second to Jean-Paul Sartre (and it was his second time taking the exam). The two had met earlier that year as they both prepared to take the exam. Sartre and his friends ("the comrades") invited Beauvoir to join their study group where she was immediately asked to lecture on Leibniz, about whom she had written a thesis. René Maheu, the comrade who introduced Beauvoir to the group, gave her the nickname *Castor* (the "beaver") because of her diligence and the similarity of her name and the English word. The name stuck all of her life and only her family continued to call her Simone.

As she relates in her memoirs, she quickly recognized in Sartre a man who was not only her intellectual equal but perhaps even a man of genius. "Sartre corresponded exactly to the dream companion I had longed for since I was fifteen: he was the double in whom I found all my burning aspirations raised to the pitch of incandescence. I should always be able to share everything with him... I knew that he would never go out of my life again" (1959, 366). Indeed, Sartre and Beauvoir were life-long companions and although the physical intimacy between the two lasted only a few years, theirs was a "necessary" relation. They each had numerous "contingent" loves but the companionship between Beauvoir and Sartre remained the central relationship for both.

After two years of living in a rented room at her Grandmother's and teaching private lessons to students, Beauvoir was ready to take a position at a lycée. In 1931 she was appointed to a lycée at Marseille while Sartre was appointed to a post at Le Havre. As the distance between their posts was quite undesirable, Sartre proposed they get married. The French government had a policy of placing married couples in the same place. Beauvoir refused however and their brief separation began. She used the time at Marseille to take extensive walking tours of the area and discovered herself as well. In *The Prime of Life* she recalls the enthusiasm with which she met this new adventure. For the first time, she was dependent on no one but herself and she discovered optimism and strength in her self-reliance (1962b, 75-94).

Her stay in Marseille was short-lived as she was transferred to Rouen the following year. While in Rouen, Beauvoir began a relationship with her student Olga Kosakiewicz. They would later add Sartre to their intimacy. The relationship significantly challenged Beauvoir's conception of herself. Olga confronted her as an independent consciousness; Beauvoir could not simply cast Olga in the role of object to her own consciousness. The "other" that Beauvoir encountered in Olga represented a threat to her freedom and her perception of herself. The trio of Sartre-Beauvoir-Olga was an attempt to live relationships with another consciousness authentically; the third person was to challenge the other two to relate to each individual involved with genuine reciprocity. The trio and its problems formed the basis of Beauvoir's novel *L'Invitee* (*She Came to Stay*) which was published ten years later. Teaching was Beauvoir's profession during this period of her life but her real passion was writing. After a number of unsuccessful apprentice novels, Beauvoir completed a series of short stories, *La Primauté du Spirituel (The Primacy of the Spiritual)*. The stories explore the impact of bourgeois ideology on a young woman's expectations of herself and others. Each demonstrates a character in bad faith. For instance, one character, Chantal (loosely modeled on Beauvoir herself), keeps a diary in which she depicts herself as a character in a Balzac novel. She envisions herself as self-determined and an idealized role model for the students she teaches. By the end of the story, however, the reader sees how influenced she is by her bourgeois values. Beauvoir interweaves narrative from another character in the story with the diary. This technique allows the reader to see into Chantal's self-deception. The collection of short stories, which also includes Beauvoir's attempt to write Zaza's story, was rejected by two publishers and it was only in 1979 that Beauvoir agreed to have it published by Gallimard under the title *When Things of the Spirit Come First*.

Although Beauvoir continued teaching through the late twenties and early thirties, when Beauvoir was in her early twenties, her focus was almost entirely on her small intellectual circle including her relationship with Sartre and her writing projects. This is notable because of the ever increasing political tensions in Europe in the thirties. Indeed, it was not until World War II that Beauvoir confronted her individualism and began to take active interest in (and responsibility for) political events. Sartre was called up for service in 1939 and this event forced both thinkers to re-examine commitments. The result was quite profound for Beauvoir. She entered one of the most productive times of her life and what she called her "moral period." In 1945, Beauvoir, together with Sartre and Merleau-Ponty among others, founded the journal *Les Temps Modernes*. Beauvoir was to remain active on the editorial board until her death. It was also during the activism of the war resistance and shortly thereafter that Beauvoir wrote and published the novels *Le Sang des Autres* (*The Blood of Others*), and *Tous Les Hommes sont Mortels* (*All Men are Mortal*), and philosophical essays *Pyrrhus et Cinéas, Pour une Morale de l'Ambiguité* (*The Ethics of Ambiguity*), and her only play, *Les Bouches Inutiles* (*Useless Mouths*).

Sartre and Beauvoir spent the war years with an intimate group of friends called "the family." As both had renounced marriage and parenthood early on, their closest friends became psuedo-children to them. Among the members of "the family" were to be counted Olga and Jacques-Laurent Bost, Sartre's former student, both of whom were significantly younger than Beauvoir and Sartre. The family frequently pooled resources and cooked together. Since she lived in hotels and ate at cafés most of her life, this was Beauvoir's only real experience of cooking, to say nothing of the other domestic duties she was forced into adopting during the war. It is significant that the future author of *The Second Sex* was so unencumbered of domestic duties most of her life.

In 1947 she was invited to the United States to lecture on existentialism at a number of colleges and universities. While in Chicago, she took the advice of some friends in New York and called author Nelson Algren. After he hung up on her a few times, she finally communicated to him who she was. Algren introduced Beauvoir to the underside of Chicago, a side few intellectuals see. It was also on that first visit in February of 1947 that Algren and Beauvoir became lovers. She writes about this trip to the U.S. in her *L'Amérique au Jour le Jour* (*America Day by Day*).

Work on *The Second Sex* also began in 1947 and culminated with its publication in 1949. One can see evidence of Beauvoir's trip to the United States through the numerous references to the situation of Blacks and women in America. The publication of *The Second Sex* marked something of a turning point for Beauvoir. Already well known for her novels and philosophical essays, this colossal study of the condition of women gained her international fame. Hailed as "the mother of second wave feminism," Beauvoir waited until the early 1970s before calling herself a feminist and actively participating in the movement. The book was met with both resounding praise and scathing criticism. Women wrote to Beauvoir expressing their appreciation for the book and how it transformed their lives; and many social conservatives of both genders vilified her for her candidness.. Indeed, *The Second Sex* will continue to be the foundation piece for feminist theory as well as an inspiration for individual women to question the effects of the social construction of gender on their daily lived experience.

The relationship with Nelson Algren lasted for nearly seventeen years, though they considered each other "crocodile husband" (for

12

Algren's toothy grin) and "frog wife" (for Beauvoir's nationality) for only the first four years. In 1951 Algren was ready to marry Simone de Beauvoir but she could leave neither her life with Sartre nor her life in France. Their relationship ended though they would remain friends for many more years. The story of her love affair with Algren is fictionalized in Beauvoir's prize winning novel *The Mandarins* (dedicated to Nelson Algren), but it was the telling of their love in *The Force of Circumstances* that lead to the ultimate break between the two. Algren was furious that their private life should be aired so publically. Beauvoir's letters to Nelson Algren were published in 1998 in *A Transatlantic Love Affair: Letters to Nelson Algren*. The most interesting aspects of the Beauvoir-Algren correspondence is perhaps the shift in tone after their break in 1950. In the early years of their affair, Beauvoir's letters focus almost exclusively on their love, their travels, and her own yearnings for Algren. After the summer of 1950, when Algren announced he no longer loved Beauvoir, a dramatic change in her letters unfolds. We begin to see her not as the "adorable" romantic but as the astute social critic and political activist living amongst some of the most notable intellectuals of the 20th century. The letters reveal the passionate and vulnerable side of Beauvoir that was largely excluded from her philosophical and autobiographical works. They also offer insight into Beauvoir's own attempt to balance work, love, social responsibility, and friendship. Simone de Beauvoir may not have been the kind of "wife" that Algren dreamed of, but there can be no denying their mutual love and literary admiration.

After the break with Algren, Beauvoir concluded that her sexual life was over. That explains her surprise when a man seventeen years her junior took an interest in her. Claude Lanzman, who later became well known for his film *Shoah,* had recently begun working on *Les Temps Modernes.* When they saw each other the attraction was mutual despite the age difference. Lanzman and Beauvoir lived together until Beauvoir won the Prix Goncourt and purchased a studio apartment in Monparnasse. She lived in this apartment until her death in 1986. The break with Lanzman was a congenial "going of separate ways" and they remained close friends.

Beauvoir won the Prix Goncourt in 1954 at the age of 46 for her novel *Les Mandarins (The Mandarins).* The novel is set in post World War II France. Two narrators alternate telling the tale of a group of intellectuals of the left. Henri obtains knowledge of Stalin's labor camps and must decide what to do with that knowledge. Anne is a psychoanalyst married to an influential writer/intellectual. They have a teenage daughter whose lover was killed by the Nazis. Anne travels to the United States and there begins a passionate affair with an American. Thus begins

Beauvoir's mildly fictionalized version of her love affair with Nelson Algren. More importantly, the novel chronicles the excitement of liberation, the factions among left-wing intellectuals, the possibilities of love relations, and the dramatic disappointment with Stalin's regime.

The next two decades of Beauvoir's life were filled with ever expanding political involvement. She and Sartre traveled extensively, including trips to Cuba (at the invitation of Castro), Brazil, the United States, the Soviet Union, and China. The trip to China launched her on another writing project. She published *La Longue Marche (The Long March)* in 1957. This is probably her worst book both in style and content (she admitted to Nelson Algren that the book was written largely to obtain money). Beauvoir praises the accomplishments of communism in China and it is clear to the reader that she either turned a blind eye to the problems of the communist revolution there or was simply naive enough to believe that the entire county was as well off as what she saw on her official visit. Nevertheless, consistent with her theorizing on oppression, she includes one chapter on the family that focuses on the situation of women (Beauvoir 1958, Chapter 3) and she frequently examines the plight of the worker before and after the communist revolution (1958, 175-184).

Beauvoir's participation in the protest against the Algerian crisis in the late 1950s and early 60s might be seen as the second "moral period" of her life. She used her notoriety on behalf of a young torture victim, Djamila Boupacha, to awaken awareness to the atrocities perpetrated by the government. In a direct application of her existentialist ethics, she asked the citizens of France to take responsibility for others and she argued that insofar as they did nothing, they were culpable in the torture and oppression of Algerians (Beauvoir and Halimi 1962). During this turbulent period, Beauvoir received phone calls threatening her life for her stance against French colonialism.

Her literary career also took on a new dimension. Beauvoir began writing her memoirs and published the first volume, *Mémoires d'une Jeune Fille Rangée (Memoirs of a Dutiful Daughter)*, in 1958. Her story is compelling not only because she was such an important figure in French existentialism but also because she reveals the life of a young girl challenging the bourgeois values under which she was raised. This volume was followed by three others: *La Force de L'Âge (The Prime of Life), La Force des Choses (The Force of Circumstances),* and *Tout Compte Fait (All Said and Done).*

In 1963 Beauvoir's mother fell and broke her femur. While in the hospital they discovered a tumor in her intestine. She died shortly thereafter. Beauvoir's relationship with her mother had been fraught with tension and even loathing at times. During her childhood, Françoise carefully censored everything Beauvoir read even going to such lengths as to clip pages together to keep her daughter from reading a questionable passage from an otherwise acceptable book. Beauvoir tells of how she would secretly read books her mother had forbidden. In adolescence, Françoise read her daughter's mail. Nonetheless, when her mother was dying, Beauvoir felt a rush of emotions, at times very conflicting, which she expressed in *A Very Easy Death*. For example, Beauvoir relates the admiration she felt for her mother while simultaneously shocked by her mother's opinions:

> Her vitality filled me with wonder, and I respected her courage. Why, as soon as she could speak again, did she utter words that froze me? Telling me of her night at the Boucicaut she said, "You know what the women of the lower classes are like: they moan." "These hospital nurses, they are only there for the money. So..." They were ready-made phrases, as automatic as drawing breath; but it was still her consciousness that gave them life and it was impossible to hear them without distress. The contrast between the truth of her suffering body and the nonsense that her head was stuffed with saddened me. (1965b, 19)

This account of her mother's death was the younger Beauvoir's way of coping with her loss but it is also a moving reflection on death, a theme with which she had long been fascinated (Marks 1973).

At the time of her mother's death, Beauvoir was just getting to know the woman she would later adopt, Sylvie Le Bon. Le Bon was a young philosophy student who asked Beauvoir for an interview. The two met a number of times and after Françoise died, it was Le Bon who encouraged Beauvoir to write about the experience. In spite of the great difference in their ages, Beauvoir and Le Bon became exceptional friends. In many ways their lives were parallels of one another. Le Bon was a philosopher and briefly taught at the same lycée in Rouen where Beauvoir had taught many years before. Their upbringing was not unalike either. Beauvoir described Sylvie as the "ideal companion of [her] adult life" (Zaza was the ideal companion of her youth) and in 1980, Beauvoir adopted Le Bon. In an interview with Dierdre Bair, Le Bon describes the relationship as love. Indeed, although the adoption was in part to provide a literary heir for Beauvoir, she also joked that "After all, it's like marriage, because you share my name" (Bair 1990, 509; cf. 505-510).

15

Beauvoir's last novel *Les Belles Images* was published in 1966 and her collection of short stories, *La Femme Rompue (The Woman Destroyed)* in 1968. Like Beauvoir's earlier short story collection, *When Things of the Spirit Come First*, the reader meets female characters who, one way or another, deceive themselves. Although both met with popular support, neither book was well received by the critics. *Les Belles Images* did not contain the social criticism on par with her previous novels and yet it aptly depicted the life of a contemporary woman trying to raise a family and maintain a career in advertising. Laurence, the main character, has a daughter, Catherine, who has begun to question the existence human of suffering. Laurence resorts to starving herself as a sort of unconscious protest against those who want to send Catherine to a psychiatrist. The first story of the three short stories that make up *The Woman Destroyed,* is called "The Age of Discretion." In it, a older scholar realizes that her new book, which she thought was breaking new ground, was really a rehash of her old ideas. Meanwhile, her husband has fallen into a slump and confesses to having had no new ideas for ages. "Murielle" is a monologue in which the title character reveals her paranoia and hysteria. Her teenage daughter committed suicide and her son lives with his father. Murielle spends New Year's Eve, the night of the monologue, in a mental sickness of self-pity and deception. Finally, "The Woman Destroyed" is the diary of Monique, a married woman with two adult daughters. Monique's husband confesses to an affair and she is shaken out of the image she has of herself as wife and mother. As the diary progresses, we learn that her husband has long stopped loving her and one daughter has moved to the United States, seemingly to break free from her mother's clutches. The diary, like the monologue, very effectively demonstrate the bad faith of the main characters. Beauvoir was often criticized for not providing a positive female character in her literature. Yet, if read with Beauvoir's philosophical project in mind, one better understands these stories as an argument for women taking responsibility for themselves and throwing off the social construction of gender that has defined them as immanence, relegated them to the domestic sphere, and limited their transcendence. Love, like other projects, must be continually chosen.

In 1970, Beauvoir published her study *La Vieillesse* which was translated euphemistically as *The Coming of Age.* The book on the situation of the elderly is modeled on *The Second Sex* and in some ways, Beauvoir argues, the oppression of the elderly is more devastating than that of women. Certainly it is more far-reaching and Beauvoir argued that the treatment of the elderly is indicative of the failures of society. She found that old age is very infrequently mentioned in literature and philosophy. Even in science, old age has only recently gained prominence as a research area, Beauvoir claims. As with all of her work, this book reflected Beauvoir's lived experience. She was 62 at the time of publication and had long felt her own mortality (Bair 1990, 539). She was even criticized for not dealing with her own old age in *La Vieillesse*, something she tried to do, in a manner of speaking, in *All Said and Done* (1972b, Preface); this last volume of her memoirs is dedicated to Sylvie. In *All Said and Done* book she declares that for her, "life was an undertaking that had a clear direction" but now in her sixties, she adds "I no longer feel that I am moving in the direction of a goal, but only that I am slipping inevitably towards my grave" (1972b, Preface).

The 1970s also marked Beauvoir's most intense period of participation in the Women's Movement. In interviews Beauvoir revised her position on socialism noting that socialism alone was insufficient for woman's liberation. She also used her name to support campaigns in favor of abortion and against domestic violence. The interviews she conducted at this time indicate her displeasure at some of the trends in feminism, in particular her discontent with theoretical positions based on deconstruction. Such abstract feminism that tries to reinvent a woman's language or woman's way of writing, she thought, was too far removed from the lives of everyday, ordinary women (Jardine 1979).

Beauvoir's life-long companion, Jean-Paul Sartre had been suffering a variety of illnesses and declining health. Beauvoir, Le Bon, and Sartre's adopted daughter Arlette Elkaïm, among others, spent much of the 1970s taking care of him. When he died on 15 April 1980 Beauvoir was devastated. She frequently recounted her fear of losing him in her memoirs and interviews. In some sense, she almost lost him a number of times in their life together. When she was involved with Algren, Sartre was deeply involved with Dolores Vanetti and Beauvoir rightly feared that he might marry her. Then in January 1965, Sartre adopted Arlette Elkaïm giving her control of his literary estate. Many commentators have interpreted this action as an implicit rejection of Beauvoir, while others simply cite Sartre's faith in youth and the future (Bair 1990, 496). Regardless of the spin one puts on the event, Beauvoir could not help but feel her relationship with Sartre slipping. An additional blow came from Benny Lévy, a student revolutionary who was Sartre's secretary during his final years. Beauvoir thought Lévy exercised too much control over Sartre and that the latter was deceived by Lévy. The final loss in 1980 was, of course, the worse. She fell ill after his death and it was only with the help of Sylvie and others that she regained her health.

Beauvoir dealt with Sartre's death the way she dealt with every major crisis in her life, she wrote about it. Her vivid account of his declining health and death, *Adieux: A Farewell to Sartre* (1985), also includes a series of interviews the two conducted. These were, no doubt, published to counteract what she viewed as the coercive influence Lévy wielded. The publication of *Adieux* met with no small amount of controversy. Beauvoir included intimate details of Sartre's physical decline. Critics accused her of seeking revenge for Sartre's seeming betrayal in his reversal of ideas, a reversal she attributed to Lévy's influence. Supporters simply held that Beauvoir continued to be true to her philosophy, she wrote about her lived experience caring for her life-long companion.

By the spring of 1986 Beauvoir's own health had deteriorated, accelerated by the alcohol habit she would not give up. On 14 April 1986 Beauvoir died. Her death sparked an outpouring of sympathy from all over the world. It was estimated that around 5000 people participated in her funeral procession and many more mourned her death. Since 1986, Beauvoir's letters and journals have been published, shining new light on the most interesting intellectual relationship of the 20th century. Included in this material is new evidence of the influence she exercised on Sartre's work, an influence she denied during her lifetime. It has become clear that the woman who changed the course of feminism also played a pivotal role in the development of existentialist morality. During her lifetime and for many years after, Beauvoir was described merely as a companion to Sartre. Only recently is her unique contribution gaining the recognition it deserves.

The rest of this book focuses on the development of Beauvoir's thought. Chapter 3, "Ontology and the Other," examines the questions of being and existing with special emphasis on the effects of another consciousness on self-consciousness. Chapter 4 explores Beauvoir's ethics found in *The Ethics of Ambiguity* and ends with a discussion of oppression and the social other. Chapter 5 presents *The Second Sex* in light of Beauvoir's existentialist ethics. The final chapter, "Liberation," offers a glimpse into Beauvoir's conception of liberation as well as her political activism.

3
Ontology and the "Other"

Like all existentialists, Simone de Beauvoir held that the individual is the source of his or her own meaning. That is, each individual existent is responsible for providing meaning to his or her existence. One adopts a project and, for authenticity, that project must embrace freedom. Failing to do so is an implicit acceptance of our status as object.

In *The Ethics of Ambiguity* Beauvoir offers a critique of Hegel that is illuminating for her understanding of the individual. She argues that Hegel makes the individual disappear. That is, the essential moment in Hegelian ethics is when two consciousnesses recognize each other. But it is the universal truth of my self that is recognized. The unique individual disappears. If the individual is nothing, then according to Beauvoir, society cannot be something. "In order for this world to have any importance, in order for our undertaking to have a meaning and to be worthy of sacrifices, we must affirm the concrete and particular thickness of this world and the individual reality of our projects and ourselves" (1948, 106). Individuality ought not to be confused with solitude or solipsism for Beauvoir. Her conception of freedom rests on the recognition of the freedom of others as well as one's own. Other people, in exercising their freedom, help me to define mine; they assist in making each individual unique through the interaction of one's project with the projects of others: "...if individuals recognize themselves in their differences, individual relations are established among them, and each one becomes irreplaceable for a few others" (1948, 108).

Given that each individual is responsible for providing meaning to his or her existence, it follows that there is no human essence or human nature. Existence precedes essence and any talk of the latter assumes the

19

active participation of the individual existent. Thus, there can be no such thing as a fixed identity for individuals. Individuals create an identity through choosing a project. As Beauvoir explains, "[a]n existent *is* nothing other than what he does; the possible does not extend beyond the real, essence does not precede existence: in pure subjectivity, the human being *is not anything*. He is to be measured by his acts" (1952b, 257).

The Other

But if each individual creates himself or herself, then a potential problem occurs when considering other people. Someone else might try to label the individual or categorize him or her, making the individual merely an object in someone else's consciousness. Beauvoir's concern with other consciousnesses is among the most important contributions to existentialist philosophy. Ontologically and ethically, the existence of other consciousnesses has proven to be one of the perennial questions in philosophy. How can we know that the other consciousness exists? How does the existence of the other as consciousness or as subject affect my project? What is the relationship between the self and the other? How can I maintain autonomy while also seeking relationship with the other?

Beauvoir chose literature as the medium with which to present her philosophy. She preferred writing literature over writing straight philosophy because philosophy spoke with "abstract voices" (1959, 219) whereas literature allowed her to communicate experience without claiming a definitive interpretation of the human condition. As she explains it, her "essays reflect [her] practical choices and [her] intellectual certitudes; [her] novels, the astonishment into which [she is] thrown both by the whole and by the details of our human condition" (1964, 319). As a result, her resolution of the problem of other consciousnesses appears in a novel, *L'Invitee.*

L'Invitee

Beauvoir's debut novel, *L'Invitee* (*She Came to Stay*), highlights the question of otherness and responds to that question in a unique fashion. In the novel, Françoise (a character modeled after Beauvoir herself) is involved in a relationship with a playwright and director, Pierre (modeled after Jean-Paul Sartre). The reader quickly discerns, however, that Pierre is the primary person in their relationship. Although Françoise muses

20

over their oneness, it is clear that the oneness is in fact her own abdication of self for the relationship. Beauvoir discusses this feminine tendency to subsume her individuality and transcendence in that of her lover in *The Second Sex*. In *She Came to Stay,* however, the focus is not on woman's situation. Rather, Beauvoir uses the novel as an exploration into metaphysics (cf. Merleau-Ponty 1964; Fullbrook 1994, 97-127; Marks 1973).

In this section I detail a number of scenes from the novel in order to better discuss the philosophical ideas presented. I begin with a brief overview and then proceed to discuss particular passages. This section is perhaps most useful when read in conjunction with the novel.

While working on *She Came to Stay*, Beauvoir used the working title *Self Defense* (Francis and Gontier 1987). The story is based on an event in Simone de Beauvoir's life involving one of her former lycée students, Olga Kosakiewicz. The real-life trio of Olga, Sartre, and Beauvoir is also the subject of Sartre's *Huis Clos (No Exit)* which was originally published under the title "Les Autres" (The Others) in 1944. In both the real life version and the version presented in Beauvoir's novel, the two older individuals (Beauvoir/Françoise and Sartre/Pierre) attempt to introduce a third party into their relationship. The idea is "to force each participant to discover himself in the scrutiny of the Other" (Francis and Gontier 1987, 146); each member of the trio would relate to one other person at a time aiming to attain perfect reciprocity (each living authentically, mutually recognizes the other as an authentic consciousness). In the novel, the third party is the younger Xavière. Gradually, the confrontation with the other leads to the destruction of the trio. While many readers comment on the destructive force of jealousy in the novel, Beauvoir's point is not to highlight the psychological effects of introducing the third but rather to examine the metaphysical implications of two consciousnesses or absolute subjects confronting each other. Unless mutual recognition of each other's subjectivity is obtained, the opposition of values and projects can lead only to annihilation of one of the consciousnesses, as the relation between Françoise and Xavière illustrates. The epigraph of the novel is revealing in this regard. Beauvoir chose the statement from Hegel, "Each consciousness seeks the death of the other," to frame her story. This theme is carried through to *The Ethics of Ambiguity* where Beauvoir discusses the inauthentic moral position of egoism, i.e., wanting to be the absolute. The existent "sees in every other man and particularly in those whose existence is asserted with most brilliance, a limit, a condemnation of himself. 'Each consciousness,' said Hegel, 'seeks the death of the other.' And indeed at every moment others

21

are stealing the whole world away from me" (1948, 70; for Beauvoir's analysis of *L 'Invitee* see Beauvoir 1962, 268-274).

As the book opens, the reader meets Françoise and Gerbert. The two are working at the theatre revising scenes for Pierre's next project, *Julius Caesar*. Françoise leaves their work to obtain some whisky from Pierre's office and while en route observes the physical aspects of the theater. She notes that the seats and the stage, etc., come into existence with her presence; when she was not there, all that she now sees exists for no one. Françoise also thinks, we are told, of her own existence: "I am here, my heart is being." This scene is significant in that it presents a literary argument for the existence of individual consciousness and for the presence of the external world while also claiming that the individual existent is the author of meaning. Françoise discloses the world through her consciousness of it. She notes that "She exercised this power: her presence revived things from their inanimateness; she gave them their color, their smell" (1954, 12). She returns to Gerbert and her work after walking through the park, realizing as she does so that "the rose-colored window would gleam in vain; it would no longer shine for anyone." Françoise alone is consciousness : "Only her own life was real" (1954, 13). This knowledge of one's own consciousness is a necessary first step for considering the existence of others. However, she is not yet *embodied* consciousness. The recognition of herself as body as well as consciousness comes with the recognition that others see her as body. That is, if I recognize myself as embodied consciousness, then I simultaneously recognize myself as potentially an object for another's consciousness. The existence of another consciousness is implied in such a recognition (cf. Merleau-Ponty 1964, 33).

Moments later, Françoise and Gerbert discuss their presence in the world and their varying conceptions of the empty theater. The theater has a different meaning for each which indicates the importance of the subjective interpretation of reality. Françoise expresses anguish at the knowledge that she will only know a little corner of the world. She overcomes this regret with the realization that the world moves with her, that is, that she is responsible for the disclosure of the world. While the indication here is that she accepts her freedom, the reader comes to understand her bad faith as we see her cede her transcendence to Pierre.

The question of other consciousnesses first arises in this early interplay between Françoise and Gerbert but does not become problematic until later in the novel. Françoise thinks "I wonder what he thinks of me..." (1954, 15), realizing that she is the subject of someone else's consciousness. Gerbert continues this theme by expressing his worry of other people. The problem he relates is that other people exist who have no knowledge of his existence. Françoise's response at this point is to deny the problem. She says of other people, "To me their thoughts are exactly like their words and their faces; objects in my own world" (1954, 17). Merleau-Ponty offers the following analysis of this and similar passages:

> If another person exists, if he too is a consciousness, then I must consent to be for him only a finite object, determinate, *visible* at a certain place in the world. If he is consciousness, I must cease to be consciousness. But how am I then to forget that intimate attestation of my existence, that contact of self with self, which is more certain than any external evidence and which is the prior condition for everything else? And so we try to subdue the disquieting existence of others. (Merleau-Ponty 1964, 29)

The real challenge of other consciousnesses for Françoise arrives with Xavière. Xavière is a young friend of Françoise who has been stifled by her family in a provincial town. Françoise encourages her to remain in Paris where she will help Xavière find a job. Convinced, Xavière agrees to stay and Françoise thinks to herself that Xavière "now belonged to her." Françoise is as yet unable to perceive Xavière as an independent existent; she is merely an object of Françoise's consciousness. At the nightclub where they discuss these plans, they observe a number of others, each of whom "was completely absorbed in living a moment of his or her little individual existence" (1954, 29). Françoise again notes that if she were to turn away from the people she observes, they "would disintegrate." Her refusal to acknowledge the existence of other consciousnesses with projects that limit and engage her project is consuming. Meanwhile, Xavière herself attempts to exert her independent consciousness. We see evidence of this in her expression of desire for absolute freedom: "I hate these compromises. If you can't have the sort of life you want, you might as well be dead" (1954, 35). There is no room for reciprocal recognition here. One consciousness conflicts with another; each subject relates to the other as object.

While we see the impending conflict with Xavière and Françoise, we also see a model for another meeting of two consciousnesses — Pierre and Françoise. As mentioned earlier, Françoise abdicates her consciousness in favor of Pierre's. This second model is a model of inauthentic reciprocity. While Françoise believes she acts freely, it becomes clear that she has subsumed her transcendence in a misguided effort to become one with Pierre. "They did not always see it from the same angle, for through their individual desires, moods, or pleasures each discovered a different aspect. But it was, for all that, the same life" (1954, 51). As the story progresses, this singularity of thought and life is challenged. Gradually we are presented with the third model of two consciousnesses interacting. When two embodied consciousnesses interact in mutual recognition of each other's freedom, then they have attained reciprocity. Reciprocity, however, requires authentic individuals, i.e., each must engage his or her freedom in the pursuit of his or her project.

Beauvoir's existential phenomenology relies on the notion of the individual as embodied subjectivity. The subject may perceive his or her relation to the body differently at different moments however. Beauvoir uses a scene in a café to illustrate the various modes of inhabiting one's body. As the scene begins, the reader is presented with a look at three different groups interacting in the café. One of the groups is the trio. "In another corner, a young woman with green and blue feathers in her hair was looking uncertainly at a man's huge hand that had just pounced on hers" (1954, 60). Elsewhere in the café, another woman was explaining to her companion that she is horrified at being touched, she cannot follow the rules of flirting. Meanwhile, "Xavière was engaged in gently blowing the fine down on her arm which she was holding up to her mouth" (1954, 60). Finally, flashing back to the woman with the feathers, the reader learns that she "had decided to leave her bare arm on the table and it lay there, forgotten, ignored; the man's had was stroking a piece of flesh that no longer belonged to anyone" (1954, 61). The scene ends with Xavière remarking, "It's funny the feeling it gives you when you touch your eyelashes,...you touch yourself without touching yourself. It's as if you touched yourself from a distance" (1954, 61). The interweaving of scenes in this passage reveals the different ways of experiencing the human body. First of all, the body may be experienced as part of one's lived subjectivity. It is that through which one experiences the world. Next one's body might be experienced as seen by others, that is as an object to another's subjectivity. Certainly the woman who found her hand in the hand of her companion makes herself an object to his subjective grasp. Her decision to leave the hand on the table is a decision to experience the body as a purely physical object, "a piece of flesh." Another manner in which an individual may experience his or her body is displayed by Xavière blowing the hair on her arm and touching her eyelashes. She experiences the body as object to her own subjectivity. She bifurcates her human experience into subject and object instead of subjective embodiment. Sartre uses the example of the woman who leaves her hand on the table as an example of bad faith in *Being and Nothingness* (cf. Fullbrook and Fullbrook 1994, 99-100). Sartre emphasizes the woman's

24

decision while, through the juxtaposition of the scene with two others, Beauvoir focuses on the woman's relation to her body. Ultimately, both analyses come to the same conclusion: the woman is in bad faith because she refuses to make a decision that would recognize herself as both object and subject/ body and consciousness (cf. Sartre 1953, 55-56).

The three characters, Françoise, Pierre, and Xavière, propose a threesome aiming to achieve perfect reciprocity among all three. But even early in this relationship Françoise begins to notice the challenges it poses. She notes, for instance, that she and Pierre do not see Xavière in the same light. This is significant because Françoise is noting a difference between her and Pierre. Their perfect "we-ness" was beginning to crack as a result of the introduction of a third. Merleau-Ponty offers this explanation:

> Françoise thought she could be bound to Pierre and yet leave him free; not make a distinction between herself and him; will herself by willing him, as each wills the other in the realm of Kantian ends. The appearance of Xavière not only reveals to them a being from whom their values are excluded but also reveals that each of them is shut off from the other, and from himself...What the characters in this book discover is inherent individuality, the Hegelian self which seeks the death of the other. (Merleau-Ponty 1964, 32)

Xavière represents the other consciousness challenging the supremacy of Françoise's consciousness and freedom. This challenge is abundantly clear in the conflict of wills. When Xavière contradicts Françoise or acts contrary to Françoise's expectations, Françoise muses:

> Was it possible that her bias in favor of happiness, which seemed to her so obviously compelling, was being rejected with scorn? Right or wrong, she no longer considered Xavière's words as mere outbursts: they contained a complete set of values that ran counter to hers. She might refuse to recognize them, but their existence was none the less invidious. (1954, 101)

When the relation between Xavière and Pierre starts to become concrete, Françoise sees the center of her world shift. "Ordinarily, the center of Paris was wherever she happened to be. Today, everything had changed. The center of Paris was the café where Pierre and Xavière were sitting, and Françoise felt as if she were wandering about in some vague suburb" (1954, 119). Françoise has discovered the existence of another subject and that that subject has the power she thought she alone had: the

25

power to ascribe meaning. This discovery is particularly troublesome because the other may define her as well as determine a world of values contrary to her own.

Françoise meets this confrontation with the other with no small amount of anguish. She realizes that the existence of another consciousness calls into question not only her relationship to that other but also to the world, i.e., her ability to participate in meaning, and her relationship with Pierre:

> She was seized by a sudden anguish, so violent that she wanted to scream. It was as if the world had suddenly become a void; there was nothing more to fear, but nothing to love either. There was absolutely nothing. She was going to meet Pierre, they would exchange meaningless phrases, and then they would part. If Pierre's and Xavière's friendship was no more than a mirage, then neither did her love for Pierre and Pierre's love for her exist. There was nothing but an infinite accumulation of meaningless moments, nothing but a chaotic seething of flesh and thought, with death looming at the end. (1954, 130; cf. 291-292)

When Françoise finally breaks down and tearfully utters that the reason for her anguish is because she discovered Xavière has a consciousness like her own, it sparks a discussion with Pierre about the possibilities of relating to another consciousness. Pierre presents the problem: "It's quite true that everyone experiences his own conscience [*sic*] as an absolute. How can several absolutes be compatible? The problem is as great a mystery as birth or death, in fact, it's such a problem that philosophers break their heads over it" (1954, 301). Two possible resolutions to this dilemma are presented in the book. The first is annihilation or death of one of the consciousnesses. Thus the Hegelian epigraph of the novel, "Each consciousness seeks the death of the other." The second possibility is reciprocity. The notion of reciprocity is one of Beauvoir's most important contributions to existentialism. In *She Came to Stay,* it is proposed by Pierre as an explanation for why he and Françoise did not face the problem of other consciousnesses in their relation. He explains, "The moment you acknowledge my conscience, you know that I acknowledge one in you too." While the reader is aware of the falsity of that statement in the context of the story, i.e., that Françoise had forsaken her consciousness for him, it is nonetheless an important revelation for philosophy. Whereas in Sartre's *Being and Nothingness* we are left with the rather pessimistic prospect of relating to other consciousnesses as war, one consciousness making the other object,

26

here we see the potential for human solidarity. Although Sartre does not preclude the possibility of authentic relationships, Beauvoir advances the project with her explicit effort to theorize reciprocity. In addition, the passage from the novel also reveals Beauvoir's conception of philosophy itself as a living exercise. For instance, Pierre exclaims his surprise that she "should be affected in such a concrete manner by a metaphysical problem." Françoise, he says, has a power "to live an idea, body and soul." Beauvoir explains the dilemma confronting Françoise in *The Prime of Life*:

Such was Françoise's first transformation: from a position of absolute and all-embracing authority she was suddenly reduced to an infinitely tiny particle in the external universe. This misfortune succeeded in convincing her, as it had done me, that she was an individual among other individuals, no matter who they might be. Now another danger threatened her, one which I myself had been endeavoring to exorcize ever since my adolescence. Other people [*autruii*] could not only steal the world from her, but also invade her personality and bewitch it. Xavière, with her outbursts of temper and spitefulness, was disfiguring Françoise's inner self, and the more she struggled, the more hopelessly she became entangled in the snare. Her own image became so loathsome to Françoise that she was faced with two alternatives: a lifetime of self-disgust, or to shatter the spell by destroying her who cast it. This latter course she took, and thus remained, triumphantly, true to herself. (1962, 269-270)

Toward the end of the novel, Gerbert and Xavière have begun seeing each other. Françoise and Gerbert embark on a walking tour and in the course of the tour they sleep together. When they return to Paris, Pierre, Françoise, and Gerbert agree to keep the relationship between Gerbert and Françoise a secret from Xavière. Françoise views this secret pact as a means of foiling Xavière's plan or desire to possess Gerbert herself. She rejoices in her triumph over Xavière saying "I've won" — "Once again she existed alone..." (1954, 375). Françoise is deluded into thinking that if her will triumphed over Xavière's will, then she would resume her place as absolute. This delusion is cracked open when she realizes that Xavière continued to have the power to define her. That is, Xavière's thoughts about her could not be stopped. Since reciprocity seems impossible with the "tyrant" Xavière, Françoise takes the only action she perceives to be open to her: Françoise murders Xavière.

Throughout the novel, there are in fact two destructive threesomes at work. One serves to foreshadow some of the events of the other. The

27

primary threesome is among Françoise, Xavière, and Pierre. The secondary and foreshadowing threesome involves Pierre sister Elisabeth, Claude, and Claude's wife. Whereas the latter tends to concentrate on the psychological effects of ceding one's freedom to another, the former, as we have seen, delves into the metaphysical.

In addition to the ontological aspects of the novel discussed above, Beauvoir carefully interweaves thoughts on morality, time, freedom, death, and society. About time, for instance, Pierre comments that "time isn't a heap of little separate fragments you can wrap yourself up in one after the other. When you think you're living in the present, you're involving your future whether you like it or not" (1954, 58). The future requires that we take responsibility for our decisions. Our current projects cut us off from other current and future projects. Because of this, we must consider carefully how we engage our freedom. Similarly, at one point Pierre explains that "what a person does and what a person is, are one and the same thing" (1954, 235). In other words, we create who we are through our projects; there is no preordained essence or human nature. There is merely the human condition within which we freely act.

It is worth noting here how little a role is played by social and political events beyond the lives of the trio. The novel is set just prior to World War II and yet the only indication of world events the reader gets until Pierre is called up for military service are the occasional newspaper headlines or discussions largely initiated by Gerbert. This is revealing both because it allows Beauvoir to focus on the metaphysical problems rather than the ethical or political issues, and because it corresponds autobiographically to Beauvoir's own life. She did not seriously address moral and political issues until the war.

As a final note, recall that the play on which Françoise, Pierre, and Gerbert were working at the outset of the novel and throughout a major portion of the text was *Julius Caesar*. A play depicting the murder of a tyrant by his best friend (among others) is certainly a fitting literary device to foreshadow the necessary outcome of the threesome. Indeed, Françoise connects the play and the fate of the threesome when she refers to the tyrannical love of Xavière. Since reciprocity is impossible with a tyrant, the only solution is murder as the epigraph of the novel claims, "Each consciousness seeks the death of the other."

Although the end is abrupt and perhaps completely implausible, both psychologically and ontologically, the novel could end no other way. In *The Prime of Life,* Beauvoir describes the writing of this final scene as a sort of catharsis:

In the first place, by killing Olga on paper I purged every twinge of irritation and resentment I had previously felt toward her, and cleansed our friendship of all the unpleasant memories that lurked among those of a happier nature. But above all, by releasing Françoise, through the agency of a crime, from the dependent position in which her love for Pierre kept her, I regained my own personal autonomy. The paradoxical thing is that to do so did not require any unpardonable action on my part, but merely the description of such an action in a book.... Rereading the final pages today so contrived and dead, I can hardly believe that when I wrote them my throat was as tight as though I had the burden of a real murder on my shoulders. Yet so it was; and sitting there, pen in hand, I felt a weird sort of terror as I set down Françoise's experience of mental isolation. Xavière's murder may look like the abrupt and clumsy conclusion of a drama I had no idea how to finish; but in fact it was the motive force and *raison d'être* behind the entire novel. (1962, 270-271)

Xavière would not admit another consciousness to exist; she would not acknowledge Françoise as a subject and thereby attain reciprocity with Françoise. To be true to her metaphysics, Beauvoir had to annihilate the offending consciousness (See also Moi 1994, Chapter 4).

The next chapter examines the existential ethics of Simone de Beauvoir. Although *She Came to Stay* is best understood in terms of metaphysics, one cannot help but wonder about the morality of Françoise's final act. In *The Ethics of Ambiguity* Beauvoir argues that "A freedom which is occupied in denying freedom is itself so outrageous that the outrageousness of the violence which one practices against it is almost canceled out: hatred, indignation, and anger ... wipe out all scruples" (1948, 97-98). Françoise might, then, be seen as justified in her use of violence against Xavière. Xavière is, after all, a freedom that is denying Françoise of hers. However, Françoise fails to adopt the genuine moral attitude because she does not take into account the projects and freedom of others. Let us turn to examine Beauvoir's ethics more carefully.

4
Existentialist Ethics

Simone de Beauvoir's ethics appear most developed in *Pyrrhus et Cineas* and *The Ethics of Ambiguity*. *The Ethics of Ambiguity* appeared in 1947 and is the articulation of an existentialist ethics. Existentialist ethics is used by Beauvoir in her analysis of the oppression of women in *The Second Sex* and also underlies many of her novels and short stories. This chapter presents Beauvoir's ethics with an emphasis on her conceptions of freedom, situation, oppression, and liberation.

In *The Ethics of Ambiguity*, Beauvoir emphasizes the ambiguity of the individual's existence. Morality arises from the individual's engagement in the world and with others. It is not externally imposed, nor is it simply part of human nature; both of these sources for morality attempt to deny the ambiguity of human existence. "In spite of so many stubborn lies, at every moment, at every opportunity, the truth comes to light, the truth of life and death, of my solitude and my bond with the world, of my freedom and my servitude, of the insignificance and the sovereign importance of each man and all men" (Beauvoir 1948, 9). The seemingly contradictory aspects of this quotation reveal Beauvoir's conception of morality as product of individual consciousness. Whereas traditional moral theory tries to escape the ambiguity by positing meaning for the individual through external sources of morality, existentialist ethics requires the individual to create meaning for him- or herself by embracing freedom; human beings are responsible for the world. Thus Beauvoir's ethics is an ethics of ambiguity — the meaning of existence is never fixed, "it must be constantly won" (1948, 129).

Beauvoir situates existentialist ethics in the tradition of ethics that moves from the individual or particular to the universal (e.g., Kant and

30

Hegel) so as to avoid solipsism (the belief that the self is all one knows or acknowledges exists). However, existentialist ethics is also significantly different: "...for existentialism, it is not impersonal universal man who is the source of values, but the plurality of concrete, particular men projecting themselves toward their ends on the basis of situations whose particularity is as radical and as irreducible as subjectivity itself" (1948, 17-18). For existentialists the meaning of a situation does not impose itself on the consciousness of a passive subject. A free subject effects the disclosure of meaning through his or her project (1948, 20).

The ontology of Sartre's *Being and Nothingness* forms the basis of the ethics of ambiguity according to Beauvoir. This is particularly evident in her use of the being/existence and in-itself/for-itself distinctions. As the sovereign, unique subject, the individual appears as a "lack of being" in order to make himself or herself "present to the world" and make "the world present" to him or her (1948, 12). "Sartre tells us that man makes himself this lack of being *in order that* there might be being. The term *in order that* clearly indicates an intentionality" (1948, 12). In other words, the move from being to existence is an intentional engagement of one's freedom. *Being* in the context of Beauvoir's existentialist ethics means identity of oneself as object or in-itself. As being, the individual statically refuses the responsibility of his or her freedom. *Existing*, on the other hand, entails the recognition of freedom and the responsibility of choosing a project that continually returns to freedom while creatively acting on the world. As both Sartre and Beauvoir tell us, however, human beings desire to be both the in-itself and the for-itself simultaneously. This impossibility nonetheless allows for the possibility that the individual will attain authentic existence: "This means that man, in his vain attempt to *be* God, makes himself exist *as* man, and if he is satisfied with this existence, he coincides exactly with himself" (1948, 12-13).

Beauvoir juxtaposes the wish to *be*, i.e., the in-itself, with the wish to disclose being, i.e., for-itself. The latter is the same as asserting oneself as freedom. "Freedom is the source from which all significations and all values spring. It is the original condition of all justifications of existence" (1948, 24). Beauvoir responds to the objection that freedom is part of our nature by saying freedom is not a thing or a quality. It must be "conquered" in order to present itself. Ontologically, one cannot help but be free. Moral freedom must be valued as an ends. The individual does so by positively assuming his or her project. That is, humans are attracted to bad faith by the lack of deep identity ontologically. The authentic person rejects bad faith by choosing freedom as an end. One cannot will oneself not free. "We, too, define morality by this adhesion to the self; and this is why we say that man cannot positively decide between the

31

negation and the assumption of his freedom, for as soon as he decides, he assumes it. He cannot positively will not to be free for such a willing would be self destructive" (1948, 33).

The importance of freedom is that the project always returns to freedom, i.e., freedom is the source of the project/choice and the content of that choice: "The truth is that in order for my freedom not to risk coming to grief against the obstacle which its very engagement has raised, in order that it might still pursue its movement in the face of the failure, it must, by giving itself a particular content, aim by means of it at an end which is nothing else but precisely the free movement of existence." (1948, 24). The opposite of this is oppression or suppression. For instance, forcing an individual to perform meaningless tasks focusing on facticity constitutes what Beauvoir calls an "obnoxious way to punish a man." Her examples include requiring an individual to empty and fill the same ditch relentlessly or requiring "a schoolboy to copy lines" (1948, 30-31).

While she clearly owes a debt to Sartre, Beauvoir also moves significantly beyond Sartre in the formulation of her ethics. Most notable, Beauvoir's version of existential ethics requires the recognition of the freedom of others. This component makes her existential ethics more applicable to social and political situations and less subject to the critique that it is solipsistic. From the very beginning of *The Ethics of Ambiguity* Beauvoir addresses the question of solidarity, i.e., "How could men, originally separated, get together?" (1948, 18).

The Moral Attitude

In the second section of *The Ethics of Ambiguity* Beauvoir presents the childhood situation as a sort of case study in freedom. Prior to adolescence, the child is deluded into believing that his or her situation is a permanent carefree existence. Adolescence breaks apart this tranquility as the adolescent suddenly realizes his or her own freedom. As a child, freedom is hidden from the individual. Slaves, women, and other oppressed peoples share a similar "infantile" state. Whereas the child's situation is imposed and temporary — adolescence is the moment of moral choice — women and other oppressed groups see little hope for unveiling their freedom. This situation is complicated in the case of women, as we will see in Chapter 5, because women are often complicit in their situation; they sometimes choose their oppressed status.

An important concept in this analysis is situated freedom. Situated freedom was Beauvoir's challenging contribution to existentialist ethics and ontology. Whereas Sartre held that absolute freedom was a possibility, i.e., that one is free in spite of the situation, Beauvoir contends that the situation within which the individual finds him or herself may limit his or her ability for transcendence. This is a condition that often affects social groups, e.g., women, Blacks, Jews, workers, more than isolated individuals. Situated freedom means that freedom is "socially mediated," to borrow a phrase from Sonia Kruks (Kruks 1995). Beauvoir explains the concept in *The Ethics of Ambiguity* using the slave and the woman of the harem as examples: "Their behavior is defined and can be judged only within this given situation, and it is possible that in this situation, limited like every human situation, they realize a perfect assertion of their freedom. But once there appears a possibility of liberation, it is resignation of freedom not to exploit the possibility, a resignation which implies dishonesty and which is a positive fault" (1948, 38). The last sentence of the quotation is important. Insofar as the individual recognizes his or her situation of oppression and does nothing about it, he or she is morally culpable. It was mentioned in the previous paragraph, for instance, that women are often complicit in their oppression. This is because often a woman will recognize the conditions of her situation that limit her transcendence and opt to maintain them rather than challenge them. The personal and social motivations for remaining in the situation appear more compelling than the struggle to overcome them.

In *Pyrrhus and Cinéas* Beauvoir says she tried to reconcile a Sartrean notion of absolute freedom with her own understanding of freedom as limited. As a result, two aspects of freedom emerge:

Liberty is the very modal essence of existence, which... subsumes to itself all external influences: this internal movement is indivisible, and thus a totality for each individual. On the other hand, actual concrete possibilities vary from one person to the next. Some can attain to only a small part of those opportunities that are available to mankind at large, and all their striving does no more than bring them near the platform from which their luckier rivals are departing. Their transcendence is lost in the general mass of humanity, and takes on the appearance of immanence. With a more favorable situation, the project makes a genuine advance, constructs a new future. An activity is good when you aim to conquer these positions of privilege, both for yourself and for others: to set freedom free. (1962b, 435-436)

The Ethics of Ambiguity moves beyond this earlier position by de-emphasizing absolute freedom and asserting a much stronger social connectedness. Situated freedom describes varying degrees of oppression or limitations on one's transcendence. We will return to this topic in the next section; however, to better understand Beauvoir's ethics it is helpful to examine her discussion of the various possibilities of attitudes toward the assumption of one's freedom. Each of the examples illustrates the movement from being to existing, i.e., each displays a different commitment to disclosing the world and freedom. I will use Beauvoir's terminology but it should be noted that the gender exclusiveness of this presentation is purely unintentional. Beauvoir's use of male pronouns is a product of the time in which she wrote and not an attempt to limit the discussion to males only.

The first attitude discussed by Beauvoir occurs when the individual fails to assume freedom; he or she does not make the original movement from being to existing. Called the sub-man, this individual tries to reject existence by refusing to will him- or herself; that is, the individual refuses to take responsibility for his or her life in trying to flee freedom. It is through acting on the world that we exist, and the sub-man fails to act on the world in his or her attempt to make him- herself being or object. As Beauvoir states, "The less he exists the less is there a reason for him to exist, since these reasons are created only by existing" (1948, 43). The sub-men are easily manipulated and often become the lackeys or members of the mindless mob in fanatic social movements.

Although the serious-man, the second moral attitude, unlike the sub-man, does at some level embrace freedom, it is done in an effort to annihilate subjectivity in an object or institution. The serious-man tries to lose individuality in the object to which he or she subordinates freedom. By positing an end and failing to will freedom indefinitely, the serious-man seeks to be identified with the object.

> If one denies the subjective tension of freedom one is evidently forbidding himself universally to will freedom in an indefinite movement. By virtue of the fact that he refuses to recognize that he is freely establishing the value of the end he sets up, the serious man makes himself the slave of that end. He forgets that every goal is at the same time a point of departure and that human freedom is the ultimate, the unique end to which man should destine himself. (1948, 48-49)

When the individual discovers that he or she is unable to be anything, i.e., to become object, "man decides to be nothing" (1948, 52), he or she tries to reject existence but is unable to eliminate it. This is the attitude of the nihilist who desires to be nothing but in doing so must deny both the world and him- or herself. The will to negation is inherently self-contradictory, manifesting itself as a presence when it tries to present itself as a negation (1948, 54). This is because the individual's presence in the world is revealed through others. One must then reject the existence of others in order to make oneself nothing. "The Nihilist attitude manifests a certain truth. In this attitude one experiences the ambiguity of the human condition. But the mistake is that it defines man not as the positive existence of a lack, but as a lack at the heart of existence, whereas the truth is that existence is not a lack as such" (1948, 57).

Much closer to the authentic ethical position is the adventurer. The adventurer makes himself a lack of being but fails in that he is solipsistic. The adventurer does not attach himself to an end, only to his action, i.e., action for its own sake. In so doing, the adventurer does not consider the freedom of others. If the adventurer shares the nihilist's contempt for humanity, he or she could become a tyrant. Nonetheless, because he or she assumes subjectivity positively, the adventurer is close to the genuine moral attitude according to Beauvoir. As she relates:

He can become conscious of the real requirements of his own freedom, which can will itself by destining itself to an open future, by seeking to extend itself by means of the freedom of others. Therefore, ... the freedom of other men must be respected and they must be helped to free themselves. Such a law imposes limits upon action and at the same time immediately gives it content (1948, 60).

Next Beauvoir describes the attitude of the passionate man. Also close to the moral attitude, the passionate man embodies something of a synthesis of freedom and its content. He or she sets up the object of passion as an absolute disclosed by subjectivity. This attitude falls short of the genuine moral attitude because the passionate man seeks possession as opposed to expressing a generous passion. Seeking to possess, the passionate man is bound to fail: "The passionate man makes himself a lack of being not that there might *be* being, but in order to be. And he remains at a distance; he is never fulfilled" (1948, 65). Françoise, from *She Came to Stay,* illustrates this attitude. Her love of Xavière is a controlling love; if she cannot have Xavière as she desires her, then Xavière's very existence announces the death of her own. Genuine love, on the other hand, loves in the other's otherness. "The case of the passionate man's torment is his distance from the object; but he must accept it instead of trying to eliminate it" (1948, 66). The goal, according to Beauvoir's version of existentialist ethics, is for two consciousnesses to exist in perfect reciprocity. This goal contrasts with Sartre's emphasis upon the fact that one consciousness necessarily makes the other consciousness an object in its own attempt to assert subjectivity.

The genuine moral attitude is characterized by the effort to exist, actively disclosing the world while simultaneously embracing freedom. Beauvoir puts it succinctly when she says, "Freedom must project itself toward its own reality through a content whose value it establishes. An end is valid only by a return to the freedom which established it and which willed itself through this end" (1948, 70). The individual adopts a project but that project itself must be a turning toward freedom. If the project ends in a static moment, then the individual has failed to attain the genuine moral attitude. For example, if an individual adopts writing as a project, then that individual must continually choose to realize existence in the activity of writing. If on the other hand, the individual writes a book and considers his or her project complete, that is, that he or she is now a "writer," then that individual has fallen into *being* as object. He or she does not embrace freedom with the content of the project itself.

We might put it in other words and say that man attains an authentically moral attitude when he renounces *mere being* to assume his position as an existent; through this transformation also he renounces all possession, for possession is one way of seeking mere being; but the transformation through which he attains true wisdom is never done, it is necessary to make it without ceasing, it demands constant tension. (1952b, 140)

In addition, however, the genuine moral attitude must entail the recognition of the existence of others: "[N]o existence can be validly fulfilled if it is limited to itself. It appeals to the existence of others...To will that there be being is also to will that there be men by and for whom the world is endowed with human significations " (1948, 67, 71). The individual's project is defined by interference or interaction with the projects of others. Similarly, the freedom of others keeps each individual from resting in one's own facticity. "Man can find a justification of his own existence only in the existence of other men" (1948, 72). Beauvoir assures the existence of other human beings and the individual's responsibility to them by making the assumption of freedom for the individual the same action as the recognition of the freedom of others: "To will oneself free is to will others free" (1948, 73).

This aspect of Beauvoir's ethics makes it particularly useful for a social ethics (as opposed to a purely personal ethics). Indeed, in the *Ethics of Ambiguity* Beauvoir turns to a discussion of oppression and liberation. It is through others that the world takes on meaning. The moral individual must disclose the world with "the purpose of further disclosure" and simultaneously try to free others. Notice that it is with the same movement that one recognizes and claims one's own freedom and tries to free others. I turn to this discussion now as it serves as background for Beauvoir's notion of the social other which frames her discussion of women in *The Second Sex.*

Oppression and Liberation

Beauvoir begins her discussion of oppression by responding to the charge that existentialism offers no concrete content for action. On the contrary, she claims this critique only arises because the word freedom has been emptied of its meaning. As she says, "we have already seen that freedom realizes itself only by engaging itself in the world: to such an extent that man's project toward freedom is embodied for him in definite acts of behavior" (1948, 78). Beauvoir illustrates this with science. Insofar as it "aspires to attain being, to contain it, and to possess it," science gives in to the serious. But if, instead, science is a free engagement aiming at ever new possibilities of discovery, then the mind projects the "concrete accomplishments of its freedom" (1948, 79). Notice that the emphasis here is on having freedom as the end or content of itself.

A situation of oppression occurs when an individual's freedom is cut off from itself by another. In this case, transcendence is "condemned to fall uselessly back upon itself because it is cut off from its goals" (1948, 81). Because only humans can confirm the existence of one another, only humans can oppress. Oppression would never be a natural phenomenon. "My freedom, in order to fulfill itself, requires that it emerge into an open future: it is other men who open the future to me, it is they who, setting up the world of tomorrow, define my future" (1948, 82). Oppression results when others fail to open the future for those they oppress but instead define them as object.

The oppressed are "condemned to mark time hopelessly in order merely to support the collectivity," while the oppressors are seemingly free to "enlighten mankind by thrusting it ahead of itself," i.e., to act creatively on the world (1948, 83). Every individual is in fact both immanence and transcendence. Oppression tries to deny that fact by

37

making transcendence inaccessible as "when one offers the existent no aim, or prevents him from attaining any, or robs him of his victory, then his transcendence falls vainly into the past — that is to say, falls back into immanence" (1952b, 255). One problem, however, is that the oppressor is not in fact as free as the situation seems to indicate. In part this is due to the efforts the oppressor must take in order to convince the oppressed that the latter's situation is natural, and in part it is because each individual's freedom is bound up with the freedom of others.

In order to prevent revolt among the oppressed, the oppressor tries to convince them that their situation is natural. When the oppressed sees their situation as natural, the oppressor has succeeded in *mystifying* them. Through degradation of the oppressed, the oppressor gains strength. Mystification keeps the oppressed from wanting liberation because he or she cannot see it as an option. Revolt, then, appears meaningless. Beauvoir includes a short Hegelian discussion on the oppressor versus the oppressed in *The Ethics of Ambiguity* that roughly matches Hegel's master/slave dialectic. She breaks from Hegel, siding with Marx, when she says "Revolt is not integrated into the harmonious development of the world; it does not wish to be integrated but rather to explode at the heart of the world and to break its continuity" (1948, 84). In other words, whereas Hegel took revolution to be a natural part of history, Marx and Beauvoir held that revolution broke up the flow of history.

Revolt is one means of the oppressed transcending his or her situation and breaking the spell of mystification. Demystification is necessary for liberation and insofar as a non-oppressed individual fails to aid the oppressed in breaking the ties of mystification, that individual is also oppressor/tyrant. As Beauvoir states, "abstention is complicity" (1948, 86; see also Langer 1994, 187). Indeed, demystification, as we will see in the discussion of *The Second Sex*, was one of Beauvoir's own projects throughout her written work.

In this sense, the struggle for liberation is universal, though Beauvoir does make a claim for epistemological and perhaps even moral privilege on the part of the oppressed in the struggle:

In any case, we can assert that the oppressed is more totally engaged in the struggle than those who, though at one with him in rejecting his servitude, do not experience it; but also that, on the other hand, every man is affected by this struggle in so essential a way that he cannot fulfill himself morally without taking part in it. (1948, 88-89)

The issue of oppression becomes more complicated because oppression has more than one manifestation. Beauvoir says we must abolish all forms of oppression and suppression. The method she advocates is to take advantage of opportunity and efficiency, and depend on each person's individual situation to respond to oppression. In addition, oppression and liberation occupy a moment in time; the means used to react to unjust situations open the future. Just as the particular individual does not exist except in his or her interaction with others, so each moment is a particular to the universal of time. "Society exists only by means of the existence of particular individuals; likewise, human adventures stand out against the background of time, each finite to each, though they are all open to the infinity of the future and their individual forms thereby imply each other without destroying each other" (1948, 122). The implications of this are quite important for judging the means used to combat oppression. Each action is a particular and must engage freedom while it aims at it (1948, 130-131). Liberation is not, then, a static state attainable at some future moment. It must be constantly won.

Inevitably, the oppressor raises the objection that he is being oppressed or deprived of his or her freedom insofar as he or she is not allowed to continue the oppressive practices. Beauvoir answers this objection forcefully by noting that freedom is not complete licence. As we saw above, each individual's freedom is defined by the freedom of others: "A freedom which is interested only in denying freedom must be denied....[T]o be free is not to have the power to do anything you like; it is to be able to surpass the given toward an open future; the existence of others as a freedom defines my situation and is even the condition of my own freedom" (1948, 91).

The next question is whether one is justified in using violence to combat oppression. Violence carries with it many negative effects. Because of the complexity of the world situation, Beauvoir reminds us, we may find ourselves taking what we view to be the most urgent liberatory action and find that we have simultaneously acted to the detriment of another cause we support. Additionally, violence "not only forces us to sacrifice men who are in our way, but also those who are fighting on our side, and even ourselves" (1948, 99). This latter theme is taken up by Beauvoir in her novel *The Blood of Others* (1974b). "Since we can conquer our enemies only by acting upon their facticity, by reducing them to things, we have to make ourselves things; in this struggle in which wills are forced to confront each other through their bodies, the bodies of our allies, like those of our opponents are exposed to the same brutal hazard: they will be wounded, killed, or starved" (1948, 99). The paradox entailed in advocating the use of violence to overthrow oppression is that it is an action on behalf of human beings against human beings. She claims, nonetheless, that the violence of denying freedom to some almost cancels out the violence one practices against it. In other words, violence may be necessary in order to confront oppression but Beauvoir maintains the position that violence is "outrageous." Necessity is the only justification and the use of violence must result in opening "concrete possibilities to the freedom which I am trying to save" (1948, 137; cf. Bell 1993).

Reciprocity

As the previous chapter shows, reciprocity as a resolution for two subjects confronting each other is among Beauvoir's contributions to existentialist ontology. Reciprocity also has important implications for ethics.

Reciprocity requires that the individual's projects be defined according to their interaction with the freedom and projects of others. This is Beauvoir's response to the objection that existentialist ethics are solipsistic. On the contrary,

...by taking the world away from me, others also give it to me, since a thing is given to me only by the movement which snatches it from me. To will that there be being is also to will that there be men by and for whom the world is endowed with human significations. One can reveal the world only on a basis revealed by other men. No project can be defined except by its interference with other projects. To make being "be" is to communicate with others by means of being. (1948, 71)

Reciprocity also lends itself to solidarity in that similarly situated individuals are grouped together according to their relation to the One or Absolute. In Chapter 3 we discussed Françoise's struggle to maintain her status as the absolute, i.e., as the one central consciousness interpreting the world. A similar struggle occurs on the level of social groups. "Otherness" of a group is a category set up by the group considering itself the self or one (the norm). Reciprocity challenges the appearance that otherness is natural while oppression reinforces it. In reciprocity, another consciousness sets up a reciprocal claim the very existence of which manifests the relativity of the self's claim to the absolute. *The Second Sex* is a sort of case study exemplifying when that reciprocity among social groups does not take place. Beauvoir asks, "How is it, then, that this reciprocity has not been recognized between the sexes, that one of the contrasting terms is set up as the sole essential, denying any relativity in regard to its correlative and defining the latter as pure otherness? Why is it that women do not dispute male sovereignty?" (1952b, xxiii-xxiv). These questions allow us to move from the otherness of two consciousnesses to the otherness of social groups.

Toward Solidarity: the Social Other

It is clear that otherness may constitute one of two possible relations. The individual may find in the other a social equal or he or she may discover that the Other is profoundly unequal (Kruks 1995, 84). The former is the condition for the possibility of reciprocity. The latter sets up the possibility for oppression. Beauvoir's ontology and ethics come together with her discussions of oppression and oppressed groups; in particular, in *The Second Sex* her discussion of the Otherness of woman illustrates Beauvoir's appropriation of Hegel's master/slave dialectic for the situation of woman, and her ethical solution of reciprocity:

> It is the existence of other men that tears each man out of his immanence and enables him to fulfill the truth of his being, to complete himself through transcendence, through escape toward some objective, through enterprise. But this liberty not my own, while assuring mine, also conflicts with it: there is the tragedy of the unfortunate human consciousness; each separate conscious being aspires to set himself up alone as sovereign subject. Each tries to fulfill himself by reducing the other to slavery. But the slave, though he works and fears, senses himself somehow as the essential; and, by a dialectical inversion, it is the master who seems to be the inessential. It is possible to rise above this conflict if each individual freely recognizes the other, each regarding himself and the other simultaneously as object and as subject in a reciprocal manner. But friendship and generosity, which alone permit in actuality this recognition of free beings, are not facile virtues; they are assuredly man's highest achievement, and through that achievement he is to be found in his true nature. But this true nature is that of a struggle unceasingly begun, unceasingly abolished; it requires man to outdo himself at every moment. We might put it in other words and say that man attains an authentically moral attitude when he renounces *mere being* to assume his position as an existent; through this transformation also he renounces all possession, for possession is one way of seeking mere being; but the transformation through which he

attains true wisdom is never done, it is necessary to make it without ceasing, it demands a constant tension. And so, quite unable to fulfill himself in solitude, man is incessantly in danger in his relations with his fellow: his life is a difficult enterprise with success never assured. (1952b, 140)

In order to move to considerations of a social group as Other instead of the individual as Other, Beauvoir must first constitute the group. She accomplishes this through the opposition of the One and the Other. The One is the essential or absolute while the Other is the inessential. As she says, "no group ever sets itself up as the One without at once setting up the Other over against itself" (1952b, xxiii). In defining themselves as the norm or the absolute human type, men have created the category of woman. Beauvoir's analysis of woman's oppression is social constructivist. She argues that woman becomes what she is through learning the expectations and assumptions about her gender. The "eternal feminine" is the set of characteristics and attributes used to create woman. Man sets up the category of woman in part according to that which he fears in himself. Man seeks to unite the for-itself and the in-itself in uniting with women. Woman becomes the in-itself for man's for-itself.

Appearing as the Other, woman appears at the same time as an abundance of being in contrast to that existence the nothingness of which man senses in himself; the Other, being regarded as the object in the eyes of the subject, is regarded as *en soi*; therefore as a being. In woman is incarnated in positive form the lack that the existent carries in his heart, and it is in seeking to be made whole through her that man hopes to attain self-realization. (1952b, 142)

Beauvoir notes that woman is not the only Other in human history. Numerous "idols" have filled that role. Woman as Other appears as a permanent category because the eternal feminine has taken on the mystifying quality of nature. That is, the eternal feminine appears as the essence of woman rather than the conditions within which individual women are raised. Beauvoir's task is to demystify the condition of women and reveal woman's transcendence. The myth of woman as Other will die out as she asserts her free being, her transcendence. Every individual is both immanence and transcendence, and each creates his or her own meaning through the projects he or she undertakes. Essence, or in this case, the eternal feminine, does not precede existence. There is nothing natural we can identify to mark women as women.

Beauvoir also talks about Blacks, Jews, and the proletariat as examples of the Other (1952b, Introduction). The oppressed groups are analogous to women in numerous ways: they are the Other to the One of whiteness, Christianity, and the Bourgeoisie. In addition, just as there is no eternal feminine, there is no Black Soul or Jewish Soul, i.e., no essence. But there are also some significant differences between the oppression of women and the oppression of Black or Jews. One of the major differences is the solidarity among the members of the group. Women have never really had a strong sense of solidarity as women. Individual women have been more tied to the men of their social class than to women of other classes or races. On the other hand, according to Beauvoir, other oppressed groups experience a much stronger sense of solidarity which springs from a memory of former days, a shared tradition, culture, history, or an historical event that bought about oppression. Solidarity may also arise from location as when oppressed groups have been ghettoized. The particularized solidarities of Blacks, Jews, or the proletariat do not contradict the universal solidarity — the responsibility each person has for every other — discussed earlier (1948, 144). Women do not constitute a united group in part because they cannot trace the historical origins of their oppression, nor can they claim a shared culture or tradition. They are isolated in single family homes and often discouraged from joining together with other women.

Regardless of which social Other one refers to, Beauvoir contends that the conditions that limit the individual's transcendence begin to be interiorized during childhood. In *The Second Sex* she presents much of the conditioning a female goes through in order to become a woman drawing on a distinction between sex and gender. Sex indicates the biological category. But biology is never interpreted unmediated by society. The subject inhabits a body through which she perceives the world but, conversely, the social world within which the individual finds herself largely determines how she will view her body. The particular social, historical, economic, and cultural context within which one is raised, then, is relevant to one's ability to exercise freedom. Certain projects may not appear to be accessible simply because since childhood the individual has been told they were inaccessible (see also Beauvoir 1974a, 35; Simons 1999, 10).

Sonia Kruks argues that these Beauvoirian innovations to existentialist conceptions of freedom (the social other and the impact of one's childhood) show that social as well as individual transformation must occur in order to overcome oppression. As she says, "there can be no effective *individual* freedom in the face of oppression, ... oppressive situations must be changed collectively for freedom to be possible" (Kruks 1995, 90).

The next chapter discusses Simone de Beauvoir's groundbreaking book *The Second Sex*. Beauvoir's work jump-started the feminist movement in the 20th century and continues to serve as both inspiration and foil to feminists around the globe. The final chapter of *The Second Sex* is a discussion of the "independent woman." While this chapter does not spell out many concrete steps women, individually and collectively, ought to take to throw off their situation of oppression, it does serve as a clarion call for a hope-filled future of gender equality. By way of introduction, it might be helpful to read Beauvoir's own coming to awareness of women's situation from *The Prime of Life:*

I began to realize how much I had gone wrong before the war, on so many points, by sticking to abstractions. I now knew that it *did* make a very great difference whether one was Jew or Aryan; but it had not yet dawned on me that such a thing as a specifically feminine "condition" existed. Now, suddenly, I met a large number of women over forty who, in differing circumstances and with various degrees of success, had all undergone one identical experience: they had lived as "dependent persons." Because I was a writer, and in a situation very different from theirs — also, I think, because I was a good listener — they told me a great deal; I began to take stock of the difficulties, deceptive advantages, traps, and manifold obstacles that most women encounter on their path. I also felt how much they were both diminished and enriched by this experience. The problem did not concern me directly, and as yet I attributed comparatively little importance to it; but my interest had been aroused. (1962b, 452)

5

Oppression of Women

Beauvoir's most influential and important contribution to 20th century thought was her colossal study of women in *The Second Sex*. This controversial book is credited with starting the second wave of feminist activism. Beauvoir used the methods of existentialist ethics to address the situation of woman. She begins by asking "What is a woman?" and finds that all of the traditional answers fail to adequately account for woman's status in society. Much of the misreading of Beauvoir's ideas has resulted from commentators who fail to take into account the structure of her overall project. She presents the outline of her argument saying:

> ...I shall discuss first of all the light in which woman is viewed by biology, psychoanalysis, and historical materialism. Next I shall try to show exactly how the concept of the "truly feminine" has been fashioned — why woman has been defined as the Other — and what have been the consequences from man's point of view. Then from woman's point of view I shall describe the world in which women must live; and thus we shall be able to envisage the difficulties in their way as, endeavoring to make their escape from the sphere hitherto assigned them, they aspire to full membership in the human race. (1952b, xxxv)

Beauvoir's stated goal is to demonstrate the obstacles constructed to inhibit woman's freedom. Her description of woman's situation, then, is not a condemnation of women, nor is it a resignation to the role prescribed for women. Rather, through the methodology of existentialist ethics, Beauvoir examines social institutions with an aim to identify the private good of the citizens; judgement is dispensed according to the concrete opportunities afforded to individuals participating in these social institutions. The description of existentialist ethics given in the introduction to *The Second Sex* is as follows:

> Every subject plays his part as such specifically through exploits or projects that serve as a mode of transcendence; he achieves liberty only through a continual reaching out toward other liberties. There is no justification for present existence other than its expansion into an indefinitely open future. Every time transcendence falls back into immanence, stagnation, there is a degradation of existence into the *"en-soi"* — the brutish life of subjection to given conditions — and of liberty into constraint and contingence. This downfall represents a moral fault if the subject consents to it; if it is inflicted upon him, it spells frustration and oppression. In both cases it is an absolute evil. Every individual concerned to justify his existence feels that his existence involves an undefined need to transcend himself, to engage in freely chosen projects. (1952b, xxxiv-xxxv)

Beauvoir finds that there is no such thing as "the eternal feminine" just as there is no such thing as a Black soul or Jewish character. That is, there is no essence that would define woman. Yet Beauvoir recognizes women, like Blacks and Jews, are oppressed. The key is to determine the cause of the oppression. Blacks and Jews, she notes, can locate an historical moment when their oppression began, they share a history, a memory of former days, a tradition or a culture, but women have always been oppressed and do not have a shared history or culture. Similarly, proletarians have not always existed but women have and have always been subordinated to men. Otherness of women lacks this "contingent or incidental nature of historical events," that is why it seems to be absolute. Indeed, women are often more closely affiliated with the men of their social class than other women. Women thus do not have a subjective attitude as women and do not have solidarity among women.

Woman's status as Other appears to be entailed in the masculine norm or absolute. When a group sets itself up as the Self or One, it creates an opposing category constituted of all those individuals who deviate from the One according to relevant characteristics or attributes. As Beauvoir argues in the introduction, "He is the Subject, he is the Absolute — She is the Other" (1952b, xxii).

But, as we saw in the discussion of Beauvoir's ethics, the blame cannot be confined to the privileged group of the One. Woman's Otherness is imposed on her but she may also collaborate in her submision. "No subject will readily volunteer to become the object, the inessential; it is not the Other who, in defining himself as the Other, establishes the One. The Other is posed as such by the One in defining himself as the One. But if the Other is not to regain the status of being the One, he must be submissive enough to accept this alien point of view" (1952b, xxiv). There is a tendency for the individual to flee his or her subjectivity, and insofar as woman accepts her status and fails to assert her transcendence she is also blameworthy for her condition:

Along with the ethical urge of each individual to affirm his subjective existence, there is also the temptation to forgo liberty and become a thing. This is an inauspicious road, for he who takes it — passive, lost, ruined — becomes henceforth the creature of another's will, frustrated in his transcendence and deprived of every value. But it is an easy road; on it one avoids the strain involved in undertaking an authentic existence. When man makes of woman the *Other*, he may, then, expect her to manifest deep-seated tendencies toward complicity. Thus, woman may fail to lay claim to the status of subject because she lacks definite resources, because she feels the necessary bond that ties her to man regardless of reciprocity, and because she is often very well please with her role as the *Other* (1952b, xxvii).

Accordingly, woman may herself be partly responsible for her status as oppressed. "If woman seems to be the inessential which never becomes the essential, it is because she herself fails to bring about this change" (1952b, xviii). This situation is further complicated when the interests of the species are taken into consideration. Man and woman are necessary to one another for purposes of procreation (1952b, xxvi). Because of this, woman's socially constructed role may appear natural thereby making it seem impossible for her to give up.

"When an individual (or group of individuals) is kept in a situation of inferiority, the fact is that he *is* inferior" (1952b, xxx). The verb here means 'to have become' in the Hegelian sense. Beauvoir is emphasizing the power of social myths, prescriptions, or expectations to form the situation of the individual. In other words, when an individual is led to believe that he or she is inferior or by nature destined for a single purpose, he or she actually comes to *be* inferior or limited to the single purpose precisely because no alternatives are apparent. The obstacles raised in order to limit the individual's freedom appear as part of the structures of nature or truth — unyielding and permanent. Beauvoir's task is to use the methods of existential phenomenology to lay bare the myths. Once the oppressed individual recognizes the fragility of the myths/obstacles put before him or her, he or she will be able to embrace freedom more completely and attain a more liberated existence.

Biology, Psychoanalysis, Historical Materialism

Beauvoir begins her search for the source of woman's oppression by examining biology, psychoanalysis, and historical materialism. Although she finds that each of these is insufficient as a causal or explanatory theory, all three are instructive in understanding woman's situation. In this section I discuss Beauvoir's presentation of each theoretical approach; Beauvoir ultimately rejects biology, psychoanalysis, and historical materialism as explanatory methods for woman's oppression while using aspects of all three to later explain woman's situation. That is, Beauvoir's position is that the "facts" of biology, psychoanalysis, and historical materialism blend with the myths of literature, religion, and culture to create an oppressive situation for women. None of these define woman's nature.

The biological term 'female' is derogatory not because it emphasizes a woman's animality but because it imprisons her in her sex. A man looks to biology for a justification of this sentiment. The male and the female are differentiated for the purpose of reproduction. "[M]an gives significance to the sexes and their relations through sexual activity, just as he gives sense and value to all the functions that he exercises" (1952b, 7). Beauvoir begins by studying the egg and the sperm and then moves on to look specifically at woman and man. At the bottom of the scale of animal life, "life is concerned only in the survival of the species as a whole; at the top, life seeks expression through particular individuals, while accomplishing also the survival of the group" (1952b, 16). That is, it is not a battle of the sexes but survival of the species that enslaves *both* male and female.

The difference between the male and the female, then, is not that of activity and passivity as others have claimed, most notably Aristotle (1952b, 24). Rather the difference pertains to their individuality versus their respective roles in reproduction with relation to the species. For the male, transcendence toward the species unites with his subjectivity in desire and coition. The female renounces her individuality for the sake of the species. The body of the woman, on the other hand, fights the pull of the species, her body becomes adapted to the needs of the egg rather than her own requirements: "Not without resistance does the body of woman permit the species to take over, and this struggle is weakening and dangerous" (1952b, 26-27). Similarly,

It is during her periods that she feels her body most painfully as an obscure, alien thing; it is, indeed, the prey of a stubborn and foreign life that each month constructs and then tears down a cradle within it; each month all things are made ready for a child and then aborted in the crimson flow. Woman, like man, *is* her body; but her body is something other than herself. (1952b, 29)

The real difference between the sexes is not the biological difference but the constructed gender difference. Man is called upon to create while woman is condemned to maintain. Both creating and maintaining serve a purpose for society but the former involves the freedom of the individual and is valued more highly than the latter.

It is true, however, that in these two processes, *maintaining* and *creating* (both of which are active), the synthesis of becoming is not accomplished in the same manner. To *maintain* is to deny the scattering of instants, it is to establish continuity in their flow; to *create* is to strike out from temporal unity in general an irreducible, separate present. And it is true also that in the woman it is the continuity of life that seeks accomplishment in spite of separation; while separation into new and individualized forces is incited by male initiative. The male is thus permitted to express himself freely; the energy of the species is well integrated into his own living activity. On the contrary, the individuality of the female is opposed by the interest of the species; it is as if she were possessed by foreign forces--alienated. (1952b, 25)

Biological facts affect one's apprehension of the world, body being that through which we experience the world. The body is a limiting factor of our projects. Biological facts, nevertheless, fail to explain the hierarchy of the sexes, or why woman is Other. "They [biological facts] do not condemn her to remain in this subordinate role forever" (1952b, 33). Similarly, violence, being contrary to custom, cannot then be the basis for domination; that is, physical strength does not justify the domination of the male. Merely understanding the body is not enough to define woman as Other. The active life of the individual within society provides the insight into the reality of what it means to be as woman. We thus need to seek further to find out why humanity has made the human female the seemingly inferior member of the species.

49

Beauvoir turns to psychoanalysis next for the justification of woman's subordination. From psychoanalysis we learn that the body is seen as lived in by the subject, rather than the body as object as seen by the biologists. It follows then that "Woman is a female to the extent that she feels herself as such" (1952b, 38). Woman defines her sex, her body by dealing with it in her emotional life. Freudianism, however, does not distinguish between emotions and sexuality according to Beauvoir.

Two essential objections to the psychoanalytic model derive from the fact that Freud based his psychoanalysis on a masculine model. First of all, Freud assumes that the woman feels she is mutilated man. Mutilation implies a comparison and evaluation. For example, the pride the boy experiences with his penis does not necessarily imply humiliation for the girl but Freud assumes it does. Similarly, the Electra complex (a female child's attraction to her father) is very vague and is not supported by a basic description of feminine libido. It is rather based on the male libido and just applied to the girl. Beauvoir points out that, according to the Electra complex, the desire of the daughter is directed at a sovereign being. Her desire does not determine the nature of its object but is rather affected by it.

In contrast to existentialism, psychoanalysis holds that a number of determinate elements explain the human story. Psychoanalysts thereby allot the same destiny to women: a battle between her viriloid and her feminine. The viriloid is the clitoral system wherein woman is identified with her father. If she remains in the viriloid she is prone to homosexuality, frigidity, or similar sexual problems; she tries to be like her father. The feminine is the vaginal system according to which woman becomes identified with her mother. Beauvoir contrasts this conception of female sexuality with the freely chosen sexuality advocated by existentialism. As she says, "All psychoanalysts systematically reject the idea of *choice* and the correlated concept of value, and therein lies the intrinsic weakness of the system" (1952b, 45).

Nevertheless, existentialism, like psychoanalysis, recognizes that sexuality plays a considerable role in human life. The key difference is that according to existentialism sexuality is a freedom rather than a determined effect of human development: "The existent is a sexual, a sexuate body, and in his relations with other existents who are also sexuate bodies, sexuality is in consequence always involved. But if body and sexuality are concrete expressions of existence, it is with reference to this that their significance can be discovered" (1952b, 45). Sexuality is only one of the aspects of the existent's "quest for being"

An additional point of contention between psychoanalysis and existentialism is that the former rejects choice in favor of determinism and "collective unconscious" which allows psychoanalysts to talk about symbolism and dream interpretation. Existentialism, on the other hand, denies natural universality but says that there may exist "general types" or common conditions. "The tendency of the subject toward alienation," to flee freedom and the anxiety it induces through looking for oneself in things, explains the "power of the penis" (1952b, 47). The phallus appears valuable, in other words, because it symbolizes dominance exercised in other areas of social existence.

Psychoanalysis, like biology, is unable to explain why woman is the Other. It gives us determinism and drives instead of choices, and fails to give us an authentic picture of the human situation. Nevertheless, Beauvoir did appreciate that psychoanalysis viewed the individual as an embodied subject. Beauvoir next turns to historical materialism for the origin of woman's status as Other.

Beauvoir was heavily influenced by historical materialism; in particular, she makes extensive use of Engels' *Origin of the Family, Private Property, and the State*. One important contribution from historical materialism is that "Humanity is not an animal species, it is a historical reality" (1952b, 53). Humanity takes over and controls nature for its own benefit; praxis, like the existentialist's project, is the practical action that acts on the world to mold the future.

Applied to the situation of woman, historical materialism reveals that woman is not merely a sexual creature: the economic organization of society affects her awareness of herself. In *Origin of the Family, Private Property, and the State,* Engels traces the history of woman according to the role/importance of maternity in society. This historical recounting argues that the changes in the modes of production brought about the shift in power from the woman in a largely matriarchal social structure to the man in patriarchal civilization. In particular, the appearance of private property in the form of land for cultivation, the domestication of animals, and the keeping of herds, amounts to the "world historical defeat of the female sex" according to Engels.

Engels' description of the private family under private property is that of man as sovereign and woman as slave. Marriage is characterized in part by the man frequenting prostitutes. Indeed, it is private property that causes prostitution to emerge as Marx argued that private property was the root of all vices. Woman also engages in infidelity (if custom allows) in the form of adultery. Although Beauvoir approves of Engels' account she notes that many important problems are not discussed. Engels fails to discuss how the passage from community ownership to private property could have come about. "It is not clear that the institution of private property must necessarily have involved the

51

enslavement of women" (1952b, 56). Part of the problem is that Engels' account concerns humans as economic beings only; it fails to account for the whole person.

Engels fails to explain the oppression of women; he merely assumes it with private property or as a class division. Woman cannot be a worker as her reproductive capacity is natural. Like psychoanalysis, historical materialism tries to categorize woman (viriloid/vaginal or bourgeois/proletarian), but these categories fail to encompass the concrete woman. Beauvoir likes the psychoanalytic view because it shows the existent is a body; she likes the view from historical materialism because the existent acts on the world (projects) according to material possibilities offered; also it shows humanity as a historical creation. But each of these is interpreted within a concrete situation involving the freedom of the individual. "The value of muscular strength, of the phallus, of the tool can be defined only in a world of values; it is determined by the basic project through which the existent seeks transcendence" (1952b, 60).

Myths

Having examined so-called "facts" and history (a section of *The Second Sex* which I do not discuss here) in an unsuccessful attempt to locate woman's Otherness, Beauvoir then turns to the myths that inform culture. Much of this part of *The Second Sex* is an analysis of "The Myth of Woman in Five Authors." Beauvoir offers interesting and sometimes scathing critiques of Montherlant, Lawrence, Claudel, Breton, and Stendhal (the last fairing the best). In this section, however, I speak more generally about her discussion of the myths that shape religion and culture.

Eva Lundgren-Gothlin argues that the Myth section of *The Second Sex* is the clearest place to see Hegel's influence on Beauvoir. More specifically, one can see the Master-Slave dialectic at work though Lundgren-Gothlin argues that woman is not the slave because she never enters the dialectic. Woman is the "inessential" (Lundgren-Gothlin 1996, Section II). The Hegelian influence is evident, for example, when Beauvoir argues that the otherness of oppression entails some similarity with the Self. That is, "otherness — is that of a consciousness separate from mine and substantially identical with mine" (1952b, 140). The existence of others enables a person to escape immanence and through some project seek transcendence. However, using Hegel's master/slave dialectic, Beauvoir argues that each consciousness, desiring to be sovereign, seeks to reduce others to slavery, i.e., to be subject while the other is object. Reciprocity is one response to this pulling toward otherness: "It is possible to rise above this conflict if each individual freely recognizes the other, each regarding himself and the other simultaneously as object and as subject in a reciprocal manner" (1952b, 140). Another response is to attempt to mystify the otherness of the other, i.e., make the otherness appear natural through the creation of myths to sustain the oppression. Beauvoir argues that man does this to woman. "Woman thus seems to be the inessential who never goes back to being the essential, to be the absolute Other, without reciprocity" (1952b, 141). But the otherness of woman also serves another function. Because she appears similar to man and yet more "natural" than man due to her reproductive capabilities, woman serves as a sort of intermediary between man and nature. Woman is, in Beauvoir's words, the incarnation of the dream "of an opaque plenitude that nevertheless would be endowed with consciousness." That is, woman "is the wished-for intermediary between nature, the stranger to man, and the fellow being who is too closely identical" (1952b, 140-141). Man is both drawn to nature and repelled from it. Man's aspirations to be *being*, he thinks, might be accomplished by carnally possessing woman; at the same time, as a free person, woman confirms man's freedom.

Appearing as the Other, woman appears at the same time as an abundance of being in contrast to that existence the nothingness of which man senses in himself; the Other, being regarded as the object in the eyes of the subject, is regarded as *en soi*; therefore as a being. In woman is incarnated in positive form the lack that the existent carries in his heart, and it is in seeking to be made whole through her that man hopes to attain self-realization. (1952b, 142)

"Women do not set themselves up as Subject" which means that the myths that are presented in religion or poetry, etc., are not from women. Women in fact adopt the dreams of men found in these myths insofar as they let the myths go unchallenged. Sexual myths are a good example of the asymmetry between the categories male and female. Myths about women, sexual or otherwise, become cemented in cultural customs and moral expectations thereby taking on the appearance of being grounded in nature or truth. "Representation of the world, like the world itself, is the work of men; they describe it from their own point of view, which they confuse with absolute truth." (1952b, 143)

Included in the nature myths of woman one finds myths about menstruation, virginity, childbirth, and death. Nature itself is often presented as a woman, witness the phrase "the rape of nature," or simply, "Mother nature." The menstruation myths are generally designed to create fear and revulsion. Menstrual blood represents the essence of femininity, it is argued, but it is that aspect of femininity from which man is repulsed. He seeks to dissociate the aspects of mother (maternal) and woman (erotic), i.e., the body which he possesses and that which gives birth to him. As a reminder that woman is natural and potentially mother, menstruation relegates her to immanence. But it is not just menstruation that man fears; the mysteries of the vagina inspire such dread that numerous absurd myths have been fostered. For instance, the older unmarried woman inspires fear because she is "flesh which is object for no subject." Virginity must be dedicated to God otherwise it is associated with a "marriage with the demon." But marriage will not free a woman from the defining/confining myths. Childbirth, too, inspires a feeling of disgust or revulsion; it similarly reminds man of his tie to nature, his body, immanence, horror, and his mother. Among the motivations for the myths surrounding woman's reproductive capacities is the realization by man that by giving birth to him, woman also announces his death. "Woman condemns man to finitude, but she also enables him to exceed his own limits; and hence comes the equivocal magic with which she is endued" (1952b, 148).

The myths are damning for woman not simply because they associate woman with immanence, but also because together they offer women only paradoxical models of femininity. Woman must be both virgin and whore, maternal and erotic. Along these line, Beauvoir discusses the myths of femininity that equate Woman and the Ideal. "Because he fears her contingent destiny, because he fancies her changeless, necessary, man seeks to find on the fact of woman, on her body, and limbs, the exact expression of an ideal" (1952b, 159). Living according to this equation requires a great deal of woman. She must make herself perfect through artificial means. She appears to attain permanence in her perfection through constant vigilance with the tools designed for her physical beauty. Witness the ever expanding market of "age defying" creams and wrinkle concealers. The paradox is that woman, being nature, is mutable but as the ideal she must be changeless: "We come, then, to this strange paradox: man, wishing to find nature in woman, but nature transfigured, dooms woman to artifice" (1952b, 159). The woman as ideal entails its opposite, i.e., she is an ideal without truth and thus is exposed in her finiteness and mediocrity. "Woman in truth represents the everyday aspects of life, she is silliness, prudence, shabbiness, boredom" (1952b, 187). In addition, her primary purpose of reproduction destroys the ideal as beauty. But beauty is not the only ideal attributed to woman. She is also entrusted with idealized virtue; in the domestic realm she is the judge of moral values. Yet she is also, paradoxically, the temptress, the embodiment of all that is evil or uncontrollable. Other ideals are even given female attributes:

> Not only are cities and nations clothed in feminine attributes, but also abstract entities, such as institutions: the Church, the Synagogue, the Republic, Humanity are women; so also are Peace, War, Liberty, the Revolution, Victory. Man feminizes the ideal he sets up before him as the essential Other, because woman is the material representation of alterity; that is why almost all allegories, in language as in pictorial representations, are women. (1952b, 179)

As is the case with all oppressed groups, the myths function to sustain the power and privilege of the oppressor. The case of woman is perhaps the most egregious in this regard. The myths themselves, however, are impermanent. They will change, Beauvoir argues, when woman is genuinely free. It is only in this freedom that woman will be able to create her own destiny instead of having the myths of patriarchy determine it for her. We saw earlier that "an existent *is* nothing other than what he does" (1952b, 257). While it is true that men must abandon their hold on the myths, women must also confront their otherness and cast off their assumption of the mystification:

> ...[T]he Feminine Mystery... is immediately implied in the mythology of the absolute Other. If it be admitted that the inessential conscious being, too, is a clear subjectivity, capable of performing the Cogito, and then it is also admitted that this being is in truth sovereign and returns to being essential; in order that all reciprocity may appear quite impossible, it is necessary for the Other to be for itself an other, for its very subjectivity to be affected by its otherness; this consciousness which would be alienated as a consciousness, in its pure immanent presence, would evidently be Mystery. It would be Mystery in itself from the fact that it would be Mystery for itself; it would be absolute Mystery. (1952b, 259)

Relationships between men and women can only be authentic if they are concretely lived. The mysteries, myths, fantasies, and dreams must be discarded in favor of each existent autonomously pursuing a project. Doing away with the myths would not destroy the romance of the relations between the sexes. On the contrary, Beauvoir argues that the romance will continue but will be founded on truth rather than falsehood.

55

This may also require a changing of aesthetics or a new eroticism as woman discovers her place among free human beings, but the new "myths" that result will enhance the pleasure of both men and women. Women must be freed from the paradoxes posed by their status as autonomous individuals and as the mysterious feminine.

Becoming Woman

The second volume of *The Second Sex* begins with the most famous quotation from the book: "One is not born, but rather becomes, a woman" (1952b, 267). Beauvoir has presented the mythical structure of woman's essence. She now shows how it is ingrained in the individual since childhood. In other words, the individual's relationship to her body, interpreted as it is through culture, must be taught. She is trained in proper behavior: how to act ladylike, how to comport oneself like a woman, and how to perform the duties of her gender — satisfying males sexually and caring for children, among others. Beauvoir's own experience of growing up as a female is revealing in this light:

> At that period of my life I associated indecency with the baser bodily functions; then I learned that the body as a whole was vulgar and offensive: it must be concealed; to allow one's underclothes to be seen, or one's naked flesh ... was a gross impropriety. Certain articles of clothing and certain attitudes were as reprehensible as exhibitionist indiscretions. These prohibitions were aimed particularly at the female species; a real "lady" ought not to show too much bosom, nor wear short skirts, nor dye her hair, nor have it bobbed, nor wear make-up, nor sprawl on a divan, nor kiss her husband in the underground passages of the Metro: if she transgressed these rules, she was "not a lady." (1959, 86-87)

Among existentialists, Beauvoir is known for emphasizing the importance of childhood on one's assumption of freedom. This is especially important when it comes to the social construction of women (1952b, 267; cf. Beauvoir 1974a, 35; Simons 1999, 10). Learning to be a woman includes the attitude the individual has to her body and this attitude, instilled in the young girl during her childhood, continues into adolescence, and is reinforced during adulthood.

Recall that the authentic assumption of one's freedom includes a recognition of the body as that through which one experiences the world.

Given this it would seem there ought to be no difference between the male and the female child learning about the world. As Beauvoir says, "In girls as in boys the body is first of all the radiation of a subjectivity, the instrument that makes possible the comprehension of the world: it is through the eyes, the hands, that children apprehend the universe, and not through the sexual parts" (1952b, 267). So from whence does gender discrimination arise? Using Lacanian psychoanalysis tempered with existentialism, Beauvoir explains the differentiation as arising from the existent's flight from freedom and desire to make himself or herself object together with the social attitudes regarding male and female genitalia. The concurrence of weaning and recognition of one's reflected image also marks the time one begins to affirm identity. By recognizing the projected self in the mirror and through mimicking one's parents, the child regards himself as an object. This is in spite of the fact that at this stage the individual "is already an autonomous subject, in transcendence toward the outer world" (1952b, 269). The independence resulting from weaning is met with fear and anguish which the child tries to appease by rejoining the mother/parent. "The nursling lives directly the basic drama of every existent: that of his relation to the Other. Man experiences with anguish his being turned loose, his forlornness. In flight from his freedom, his subjectivity, he would fain lose himself in the bosom of the Whole" (1952b, 268). In fleeing the initial separation from the mother, the child seeks justification through others who bestow existence but their gaze is informed by social standards. Herein lies the primary moment when the little girl recognizes herself as different from the little boy. Beauvoir refers to the moment of gender differentiation as a "second weaning." Both the boy and the girl are further deprived of the mother's caresses but the little boy experiences the loss more consistently. He gains approval by being independent while the little girl gains approval insofar as she learns the coquetry of femininity. She still receives embraces which further protect her from the solitude of independence.

The superiority of boys is embodied in the penis. Beauvoir, however, rejects the essentialism and determinism of traditional psychoanalysis. Instead, the pride associated with the penis arises in response to the pride those around him express at the male child's genitalia. He is taught pride in his manhood which is identified with the penis/phallus. It follows, then, that penis envy is not an essential component of the development of the female. She learns to envy the penis as somehow embodying the male power or prestige because it is the only significant difference between her and the boy and others attribute so much importance to it. Often, according to Beauvoir's research, this jealousy is concretely expressed through the difference in urinary functions between the sexes. The little girl is envious of the ease and simplicity with which the little boy urinates. She, on the other hand, is forced to uncover herself, to expose her bottom. Once again, she is taught by those around her the shame associated with her body and the inverse pride associated with the body of her male counterpart.

While the male child has the penis as alter ego, the female child is given a doll (and later the child). This lends to the female narcissistic tendency according to Beauvoir. The doll is a passive object representing the whole body (1952b, 278). As such, "the little girl will be led to identify her whole person....While the boy seeks himself in the penis as an autonomous subject, the little girl coddles her doll and dresses her up as she dreams of being coddled and dressed up herself; ...she thinks of herself as a marvelous doll" (1952b, 278-279). The girl is encouraged in this identification with the doll to such an extent that a tension develops between herself as autonomous and herself as object. The encouragement is found in social mores dictating proper feminine behavior and social standards of beauty. "Thus a vicious circle is formed; for the less she exercises her freedom to understand, to grasp and discover the world about her, the less resources will she find within herself, the less will she dare to affirm herself as subject" (1952b, 280). But the female is not free of blame in this oppressive process. Given the tendency of the existent to flee his or her subjectivity, the young girl may delight in passivity — a delight that is reinforced by the accolades she receives from parents, teachers, and friends.

The key to understanding Beauvoir's analysis of woman's situation is that the individual is a human being first. Society, with all of its myth-making tools, constructs woman out of raw human potential by limiting her freedom and she responds often with resignation. This process begins not with the differentiation of sexes but with the assignment of genders. Woman's oppressed situation, then, is learned since early childhood. But childhood need not be the training ground for an oppressed adulthood. In *The Ethics of Ambiguity* Beauvoir appeals to Rousseau's *Emile* for a model of non-oppressive childhood. Rousseau outlined the education of the "man of nature" as opposed to the individual constrained by social mores. One must consider the child a human person with a right to freedom. As Beauvoir says, "practicing raising a child as one cultivates a plant which one does not consult about its need is very different from considering it as a freedom to whom the future must be opened" (1948, 142). Ironically, Rousseau's suggestion for rearing the female child, Sophie, is replete with the very structures of femininity Beauvoir deplores.

As the child moves into adolescence each new development deepens the shame in her body as flesh. Menstruation, breasts, sexual urgings, all conspire to reinforce her otherness.

> We are now acquainted with the dramatic conflict that harrows the adolescent girl at puberty: she cannot become "grown-up" without accepting her femininity; and she knows already that her sex condemns her to a mutilated and fixed existence, which she faces ... under the form of an impure sickness and a vague guiltiness. Her inferiority was sensed at first merely as a deprivation; but the lack of a penis has now become defilement and transgression. So she goes onward toward the future, wounded, shameful, culpable. (1952b, 327)

Sexual Initiation and Lesbianism

It is no surprise that the man and the woman experience their sexuality differently. Society has informed how the male and the female experience their bodies. The man, in sexuality, maintains his transcendence.

> ...with penis, hands, mouth, with his whole body, a man reaches out toward his partner, but he himself remains at the center of this activity, being, on the whole, the *subject* as opposed to *objects* that he perceives and *instruments* that he manipulates; he projects himself toward the other without losing his independence; the feminine flesh is for him a prey, and through it he gains access to the qualities he desires, as with any object. (1952b, 371)

The woman, on the other hand, passively enacts her service to the species. As we have seen, her physiological difference from man is interpreted as a lack, or in the most extreme form, as a deformity. Shame accompanies her experience of her body. Social and moral conditions also conspire to control woman's sexual experience. Patriarchy, whether through custom or law, has dictated chastity for women while allowing men to be more or less sexually free. Given these conditions, Beauvoir argues, it is understandable that a woman may meet her sexual initiation with fear. Penetration is viewed as a tearing, a violation, or a hostile intrusion (1952b, 383, 387). If it happens outside of a monogamous marriage, sexual intercourse is viewed by society as "soiling" the woman, she is "damaged goods." No similar censure applies to male premarital sexual experience. But sexuality need not be based on such inequality of judgement and experience. The availability of contraception, Beauvoir argues, "is a great step in the sexual emancipation of women" (1952b, 387). In addition, sexual initiation (and subsequent sexual experiences), if undertaken in reciprocity, can be mutually pleasurable. The trauma can be avoided if the couple acts genuinely, free from the social prescriptions of the "wedding night" or "first time." The woman must learn to overcome her modesty and relate to her body as subject; the man must help her overcome her inferiority complex. Even beyond the immediacy of the event, however, sexual relations can only be undertaken in equality if there is real social equality as well.

Some women, according to Beauvoir, opt to reclaim their sexuality outside of the "standard fashion" turning instead to homosexuality. Understanding Beauvoir's position on lesbianism rests on understanding her rejection of identity as *being*. To *be* a lesbian is to close oneself off from the responsibility of freedom. If one exists as lesbian, on the other hand, then the individual continually chooses the love of another woman over that of a man and can, at any point, choose otherwise. This latter position describes an authentic lifestyle as a lesbian. Beauvoir warns, however, that in throwing off the prescriptions of male oppression and femininity some lesbians become "imprisoned" in the identity of lesbian. She also warns against the "noisy zealots" who discredit lesbianism via their too obvious actions as lesbians — they reinforce society's view that feminine homosexuality is a vice.

To further support this distinction, Beauvoir mentions that psychiatrists and sexologists confirm that lesbians are like other women in anatomical constitution. Anatomy and hormones only set the situation, they "do not set the object toward which the situation is to be transcended" (1952b, 405). We are not, in other words, confined by our biology. Similarly, Beauvoir rejects the psychoanalytic explanation of lesbianism as a state of arrested development. Psychoanalysts mistakenly view female sexuality as symmetrical to male sexuality. This is a mistake on at least two fronts. First, psychoanalysis is wrong to define the proper or improper development of sexuality deterministically. Secondly, the conflation of female and male sexuality ignores the biological differences and, more importantly for Beauvoir, the social situations of each.

The existentialist view of homosexuality directly challenges the determinism posed by psychoanalysis:

The history of an individual is not a fatalistically determined progression: at each moment the past is re-appraised, so to speak, through a new choice, and the 'normality' of the choice gives it no preferred value — it must be evaluated according to its authenticity. Homosexuality can be for woman a mode of flight from her situation or a way of accepting it. (1952b, 406)

Two socially identified types of lesbian are the masculine lesbian and the feminine lesbian. The masculine lesbian aims to attain certain values that are in fact human values but which have been associated with masculinity. Thus, when she pursues human projects and goals, she is described as masculine. The key to understanding this is that society views it *natural* for women to take on feminine, i.e., passive or immanent, characteristics. As a result, many creative, intelligent women choose lesbianism because they do not wish to waste their energies on "playing the feminine role or in struggling with men" (1952b, 410). Lesbians obtain a "masculine cast" not because of their eroticism but because of the responsibilities they must take up in refusing men.

The feminine lesbian, unlike the masculine lesbian who refuses to make herself object, desires to cultivate her femininity/object status. "To be willing to be changed into a passive object is not to renounce all claim to subjectivity: woman hopes in this way to find self-realization under the aspect of herself as a thing; but then she will be trying to find herself in her otherness, her alterity" (1952b, 416).

Regardless of the type of lesbian or whether or not the lifestyle is adopted authentically, it is wrong to try to differentiate between the homosexual woman and the heterosexual woman. Homosexuality is freely "chosen in a certain situation" (1952b, 424). Like all human activity, it can be chosen in bad faith or authenticity. Physiology, psychological history, and social circumstances all contribute to the explanation of lesbianism for the individual but none is the determining factor. Only a free choice can determine one's sexual preference at any given time, according to Beauvoir. Her own life bears witness to this conception of lesbianism. While she had a few well publicized romances with men, she had many relations with women (Beauvoir 1991).

Having discussed the formation of woman, Beauvoir advances to her situation. Woman is continually reinforced in her role as immanence through her status as wife and mother. I will focus primarily on Beauvoir's descriptions of marriage, motherhood, and prostitution as these are among the most controversial chapters of *The Second Sex* and the most revealing accounts of woman's oppressed condition. Beauvoir is quick to point out, however, that the situation is not a necessary one. Woman can break free from her oppression by living her relationships concretely instead of via prescribed roles, by assuming her freedom, and by working. But the individual woman cannot attain liberation in isolation. Social transformation necessarily accompanies the struggles to transform individual lives.

Marriage and Housework

Marriage has been quite a different experience for man and for woman. Because man is socially independent and a complete individual, his destiny has not been limited to family life. Rather, his existence is justified by what he produces and what he contributes to the society. Woman, on the other hand, has traditionally been offered marriage as her sole destiny and individual fulfillment. Beauvoir argues that being thus confined to the domestic and reproductive role, woman is not accorded equal dignity with man. "The young girl's freedom of choice has always been much restricted; and celibacy — apart from the rare cases in which it bears a sacred character — reduced her to the rank of parasite and pariah; marriage is her only means of support and the sole justification of her existence." (1952b, 427) As we saw in the section on biology, woman is the servant of the species; she is enslaved to the family. Evidence of this enslavement is found in the very language and ritual of the marriage ceremony: she is given in marriage. Once in the marriage, the evidence of enslavement continues. As Beauvoir presents the situation, women must provide society with children, satisfy a male's sexual needs, and take care of his household. These duties are regarded as a service rendered by the woman in exchange for support, gifts, and a marriage settlement. Echoing Hegel, Beauvoir writes:

> Since the husband is the productive worker, he is the one who goes beyond family interest to that of society, opening up a future for himself through co-operation in the building of the collective future: he incarnates transcendence. Woman is doomed to the continuation of the species and the care of the home — that is to say, to immanence. The fact is that every human existence involves transcendence and immanence at the same time; to go forward, each existence must be maintained, for it to expand toward the future it must integrate the past, and while intercommunicating with others it should find self-confirmation. (1952b, 429-430)

Arranged marriages are perhaps the extreme example of the passivity of the woman in her situation: "she *is* married, *given* in marriage by her parents" (1952b, 429). Although at the time of the writing of *The Second Sex* arranged marriages were no longer the custom in France, during

Beauvoir's adolescence they were still the norm among the bourgeoisie. Indeed, Beauvoir's best female friend Elizabeth Le Coin (Zaza) was destined for an arranged marriage prior to her untimely death. In a sense, Beauvoir argues, "arranged marriages" persist in the traditions of the social classes where parents restrict their children's social circles or keep a close guard on their children's friends. In any case, until there is a live option not to marry, a young woman cannot really be free (1952b, 433). Interestingly, it is also to Zaza that Beauvoir attributes the notion of a marriage of convenience equaling prostitution (1959, 160).

The implications for woman's erotic life are telling. Woman has "no right to any sexual activity apart from marriage" (1952b, 435). Social mores are such that premarital or extramarital sexual intercourse is viewed as acceptable or even expected for men but not for women. Because of the connection between the erotic function and the reproductive function in woman, a connection not found in men, marriage lends an ethical status to woman's erotic life and thereby intends to suppress it.

While it is desirable to unite love and marriage, or integrate sexuality and marriage, it is not often possible, Beauvoir argues, simply because of the social prescriptions that confine woman's physical and psychological pursuits. A woman's pleasure is wrapped up in her entire psychological situation yet her situation is complicated by paternalistic ethics that demand virginity from her. The individual good of the woman is sacrificed for the good of society which results in a perception of sexual relations as purely animalistic rather than expressions of freedom and love. With the liberation of women, sexuality would be united with love and monogamy would be continuously chosen rather than institutionalized. "A humanist morality would require that all life experience have a human meaning, that it be infused with liberty; in a genuinely moral erotic relation there is free assumption of desire and pleasure, or at least a moving struggle to regain liberty in the midst of sexuality; but this is possible only when the other is recognized *as an individual*, in love or in desire." (1952b, 440)

Beauvoir also discusses some of the more detailed aspects of marriage. For instance, she examines the social customs of the wedding night or first initiation into sexual intercourse. The wedding night appears to turn sexual intercourse into a duty. It becomes a test for both parties inhibiting their ability to act generously toward the other. Woman's erotic interests are virtually killed by the efforts to regularize them. The paradox is that women's erotic capabilities are virtually limitless. "Marriage is obscene in principle in so far as it transforms into rights and duties those mutual relations which should be founded on a spontaneous urge; it gives an instrumental and therefore degrading character to the two

63

bodies in dooming them to know each other in their general aspect *as* bodies, not *as* persons." (1952b, 444)

Beauvoir succinctly summarizes her philosophical opposition to marriage in the following:

...to conserve and continue the world as it is seems neither desirable nor possible. The male is called upon for action, his vocation is to produce, fight, create, progress, to transcend himself toward the totality of the universe and the infinity of the future; but traditional marriage does not invite woman to transcend herself with him; it confines her in immanence, shuts her up within the circle of herself. She can thus propose to do nothing more than construct a life of stable equilibrium in which the present as a continuance of the past avoids the menaces of tomorrow. (1952b, 448)

Thus Beauvoir is led to a discussion of the material conditions of woman's situation. The house stands for permanence, stability, and separation from the world. While men regard the objects that surround him as instruments, the woman regards it as a source of meaning: by decorating her house she is giving her interior meaning and value. The home becomes the only reality the woman knows, it is the center of the world. Similarly, the child is the embodiment of the future "in portable form" (1952b, 450). "Because she *does* nothing, she eagerly seeks self-realization in what she *has*" (1952b, 451). Housework is a simple perpetuation of the present and is compared to the torture of Sisyphus who was condemned to endlessly roll a rock up hill only to have it fall back again. Housework is drudgery that allows a woman to busy herself and forget her own existence. Only if the houseworker also performs creative or productive work is housework more naturally integrated into the course of life and viewed as merely a passing negative. "What makes the lot of the wife-servant ungrateful is the division of labor which dooms her completely to the general and the inessential" (1952b, 454).

With increasing economic equality for women and more men sharing in the duties of the domestic sphere, Beauvoir argues, the institution of marriage is being transformed. Marriage is a union freely entered by two independent persons. The parties of the marriage contract have personal and reciprocal obligations. However, any reciprocal relationship must involve human persons at liberty to pursue their individual transcendence.

Motherhood/Maternity

The chapter on motherhood in *The Second Sex* is among the most controversial chapters. Beauvoir opens the chapter by claiming that "It is in maternity that woman fulfills her physiological destiny; it is her natural 'calling,' since her whole organic structure is adapted for the perpetuation of the species" (1952b, 484). Yet Beauvoir rapidly moves to a discussion of abortion and contraception, i.e., artificial means of preventing motherhood. The two-fold irony here is important. First of all, Beauvoir notes that the reproductive function has long been a matter of choice rather than biological chance. Contraceptives, whether practiced openly or covertly, aid the element of choice against the pulls of "nature" for women. In other words, her opening sentence is an ironic statement of the social prescriptions on women that are based on a perceived understanding of the natural function of women to reproduce. That is part of the mystification that society constructs making woman's "destiny" as mother appear natural. Secondly, by focusing so much attention early in the chapter not on motherhood but on abortion and contraception, Beauvoir openly challenges those social prescriptions and also reveals that abortion is widespread enough to be considered a part of woman's situation. Her intent is not to deny the potential of motherhood to be a meaningful activity, it is to deny that motherhood is part of woman's nature (cf. Simons 1989, 18-19). A woman must choose to be a mother and must continually choose to have a relationship with her child/children. To better understand Beauvoir's point, I discuss this chapter in some detail.

Abortion, Beauvoir argues, reveals woman's situation as subjected to male social, economic, political, and moral structures. Economically, a woman's circumstances affect the moral aspect of abortion; the wealthier the woman — the more emancipated — the less she feels society's reproving eyes. Referring to abortion as something of a "class crime," Beauvoir points out that poverty, overcrowding, and a need to work outside of the home are among the most frequent causes of abortion. Similarly, the ordeal of abortion varies according to the means available to the woman. Women with money may find it easier to obtain a "therapeutic abortion," i.e., recommended by their doctor. The wealthy woman also has access to travel, better care, and more expedient procedures. Those women without financial means find themselves isolated; often they are forced to wait until a fairly advanced stage of pregnancy thereby increasing the risks; some even prefer suicide or infanticide; some women severely injure themselves by appealing to "self-inflicted remedies" like knitting needles or oral cleaning solutions.

Morally, abortion challenges the moral system prescribed by men precisely because it denies that woman is destined to bear children: "The woman who has recourse to abortion is disowning feminine values, her values, and at the same time is in most radical fashion running counter to the ethics established by men" (1952b, 491). Additionally, a man who asks a woman to seek an abortion is "exposing the hypocrisy of the masculine moral code." Universally men forbid abortion but "individually they accept it as a convenient solution" (1952b, 491). Further, society defends the rights of the embryo but cares little about the child after it is born. Beauvoir illustrates this point by noting that children suffer all kinds of abuse at the hands of adults/parents but people turn the other way because such matters are viewed as private.

Beauvoir's point is in part that "Contraception and legal abortion would permit woman to undertake her maternities in freedom" (1952b, 492). It must be remembered that Beauvoir does think that maternity can be undertaken authentically. The problem is that society imposes a "maternal instinct" on women. According to existentialist ethics, however, there is in fact no maternal instinct but only a conscious decision on the part of woman to mother.

Under the imposition of the eternal feminine, pregnancy might be experienced as an invasion of the woman's body. She might view the fetus as a parasite. The pain and sickness associated with pregnancy and childbirth will depend on her degree of independence from the social mores of womanhood. The woman chooses her reaction to the pregnancy and thus women feel it differently. Implicitly drawing on Hegel's analysis of externalization found in the *Phenomenology*, Beauvoir describes the pregnancy:

> She feels it as at once an enrichment and an injury; the fetus is a part of her body, and it is a parasite that feeds on it; she possesses it, and she is possessed by it; it represents the future and, carrying it, she feels herself vast as the world; but this very opulence annihilates her, she feels that she herself is no longer anything. A new life is going to manifest itself and justify its own separate existence, she is proud of it; but she also feels herself tossed and driven, the plaything of obscure forces. It is especially noteworthy that the pregnant woman feels the immanence of her body at just the time when it is in transcendence: it turns upon itself in nausea and discomfort; it has ceased to exist for itself and thereupon becomes more sizable than ever before. The transcendence of the artisan , of the man of action,

contains the element of subjectivity; but in the mother-to-be the antithesis of subject and object ceases to exist; she and the child with which she is swollen make up together an equivocal pair overwhelmed by life. Ensnared by nature, the pregnant woman is plant and animal..... (1952b, 495)

This is followed by the explicit renunciation of pregnancy as a creative act — the baby makes itself within her, she does not make it. Motherhood, however, may be a creative meaningful act. Because Beauvoir spends most of the chapter on motherhood discussing the pitfalls of pregnancy and the psychological damage mothers inflict on their male and female children, many commentators have overlooked Beauvoir's central point. She argues that motherhood can be a meaningful, creative act, if it is undertaken in freedom. She adds that it will be more fulfilling for both mother and child if the woman participates in the social, economic, and political world. Consider the following quotation:

We have seen that woman's inferiority originated in her being at first limited to repeating life, whereas man invented reasons for living more essential, in his eyes, than the not-willed routine of mere existence; to restrict woman to maternity would be to perpetuate this situation. She demands today to have a part in that mode of activity in which humanity tries continually to find justification through transcendence, through movement toward new goals and accomplishments; she cannot consent to bring forth life unless life has meaning; she cannot be a mother without endeavoring to play a role in the economic, political, and social life of the times. ... On the contrary, the woman who works — farmer, chemist, or writer — is the one who undergoes pregnancy most easily because she is not absorbed in her own person; the woman who enjoys the richest individual life will have the most to give her children and will demand the least from them; she who acquires in effort and struggle a sense of true human values will be best able to bring them up properly. (1952b, 524-525)

Prostitution

Following Engels' argument in *The Origin of the Family, Private Property, and the State,* Beauvoir contends that prostitution is correlated with monogamous marriage. Monogamy and, more generally,

67

social/sexual mores, require the chastity of women primarily for inheritance reasons. This patriarchal morality does not, however, hold men to the same standards of chastity as women. Prostitution arises as a response to the relaxed standards of morality for man and the stifling aspects of marriage. Marriage, as we saw above, takes on the aspect of slavery for the woman and one quickly sees what little role love plays in the marriage union.

Among the social arguments in favor of prostitution is that it is necessary to sacrifice one part of the female sex in order to save the other part. That is, if some women makes themselves readily available to men sexually, then other women are preserved in their virginity and/or chastity. Prostitutes are morally adapted to their lifestyle; they are integrated into a society that demands their services. Yet, as Beauvoir points out, again appealing to Engels, economically, the married woman and the prostitute are not that different. The former sells herself to one man indefinitely, the other to many men "who pay her by the piece." Both exchange sexual service for economic compensation of some sort. There is a crucial difference between the wife and the prostitute though. The wife still retains her respect in society while the prostitute remains enslaved:

> The great difference between them is that the legal wife, oppressed as a married woman, is respected as a human being; this respect is beginning definitely to check the oppression. So long as the prostitute is denied the rights of a person, she sums up all the forms of feminine slavery at once. (1952b, 556)

The reasons for entering prostitution are numerous. The primary motivation Beauvoir cites is the economic one. Women enter prostitution because it is a profession that is open and pays well in a world of unemployment and poverty. Certainly a woman can make a living in other ways, but she chooses prostitution because it promises a better life or provides money or resources quickly. Beauvoir offers a scathing social critique here; she condemns the society in which prostitution seems "the least repellent [choice] to many women" (1952b, 557). Similarly, once in the profession Beauvoir notes that "it is common for her to be kept in the business against her will" by a pimp or "protector" (1952b, 560).

Other reasons a woman enters prostitution concern her relationship with sexuality or her body. Many girls, Beauvoir argues, find it natural to yield their bodies to anyone after they have lost their virginity. They find themselves detached from their bodies or they may instead respond to the trauma of defloration with passivity in sexual relations. Some girls

68

get into prostitution following prostitution fantasies. They easily slip from dreams to acts. Or perhaps the young girl responds to the abandonment by her first lover by giving herself to many others. "Now that she no longer belongs to one man, she feels she can give herself to all" (1952b, 558). Lovers themselves may even suggest she prostitute herself as a means of earning money. Often the prostitute is in love with her pimp. Beauvoir explains that "...it is through love that she got into the work, and justifies it. In her environment man is enormously superior to woman, and this setting apart favors a kind of love-religion, which explains the passionate abnegation of certain prostitutes" (1952b, 561). More likely, the prostitute remains under the control of her pimp through fear of violent reprisals should she leave.

As we have seen throughout *The Second Sex*, women are often responsible for their own oppression, both individually and as a social group. The same might be said for prostitution as well. Women might be led into prostitution by another woman, either as a love or as a madam. But other women/other prostitutes also serve as "chums": "Because their relations with one half of humanity are of a commercial kind and because society as a whole treats them as pariahs, prostitutes have a close solidarity among themselves....they profoundly need one another in order to form a counter-universe in which they regain their human dignity" (1952b, 562).

Thus far Beauvoir has not strayed far beyond classic and contemporary explanations of prostitution though she does focus more on the psychological make-up of individual prostitutes rather than the social conditions that necessitate the existence of prostitution as a profession. She quickly moves into a much more controversial position with her discussion of the hetaira versus the common prostitute. The common prostitute, according to Beauvoir, practices her trade in her "pure generality -- as woman." The hetaira, on the other hand, practices her trade as an individual, to gain recognition for herself. "Hetaira" is used by Beauvoir "to designate all women who treat not only their bodies but their entire personalities as capital to be exploited" (1952b, 567). In other words, the hetaira intentionally makes herself the embodiment of the eternal feminine. "She yields Woman over to the dreams of man, who repays her with wealth and fame" (1952b, 565). The movie star is the latest version of hetaira. In some sense, by making herself what man wants, the hetaira is very powerful. She exercises a sort of charm over men and is often able to bend them to her will. The hetaira, however, is not transcendence, she does not reveal the world, there is no creativity in her work that opens the future. "Offering herself for the approbation of her admirers, she does not repudiate that passive femininity which

69

dedicates her to man: she endues it with a magical power that enables her to catch the men in the snare of her presence and batten off them; she engulfs them along with her in immanence" (1952b, 567)

> ...the attitude of the hetaira is more or less analogous to that of the adventurer; like him, she is often midway between *the serious* and *adventure*, properly so called; her aim is toward respectable ready-made values, such as money and fame; but she prizes the fact of their attainment as highly as their possession, and, in the end, to her the supreme value is her subjective success. (1952b, 573)

Though she may exercise some influence on the men she is attached to, the prostitute/hetaira is emancipated only on the erotic level. She makes an instrument of man by making him pay. She is nonetheless an Other cut off from her transcendence.

Justifications: Narcissist and Woman in Love

Beauvoir claims that liberation must be collective and "it requires first of all that the economic evolution of woman's condition be accomplished" (1952b, 627). There are, however, some women who seek to achieve salvation solitarily. "They are attempting to justify their existence in the midst of their immanence — that is, to realize transcendence in immanence" (1952b, 267-28). The "Justifications" section of *The Second Sex* details three of the strategies women use to turn their oppression into "heaven": the narcissist, the woman in love, and the mystic. Using examples from Beauvoir's novels and short stories, I discuss the narcissist and the woman in love and only briefly touch on the mystic in this section.

The Narcissist is the woman who finds the object of her love in herself, the subject. That is, love requires both a subject (the lover) and an object (the loved). The narcissist unites these two in her own person. The result, however, is a skewed assumption of individual freedom that is an embrace of immanence rather than a striving for transcendence. "Narcissism is a well-defined process of identification, in which the ego is regarded as an absolute end and the subject takes refuge from himself in it" (1952b, 629). The paradox is that the narcissist seeks value from a world that she must consider valueless because she is the only one who counts in her opinion.

One reason a woman turns to narcissism is that she feels frustrated as a subject. "She is occupied, but she *does* nothing"; masculine activities are not open to her (1952b, 629). Because she is incapable of forgetting her ego and give of herself, she is incapable of a genuine love affair. The narcissist needs society; she needs to exhibit herself through clothes, conversation, or even on the stage. "If she avoids the tyranny of an individual man, she accepts the tyranny of public opinion. This tie that binds her to others implies no reciprocity of exchange, for she would cease to be a narcissist if she sought to obtain recognition in the free estimate of others while recognizing such estimation as an end to be gained through activities" (1952b, 640).

Since puberty, woman has known that her own body is passive and desirable; she identifies herself with her body. As a child, the girl turns to her doll as the self embodied in an other. As an adolescent and adult, the woman turns to her mirror. A man's physical beauty suggests transcendence; woman's suggests the passivity of immanence — this is why she can be "captured" as object in the mirror. "What contents the soul is the fact that, while the mind will have to prove itself, the contemplated countenance is there, today, a given fact, indubitable. All the future is concentrated in that sheet of light, a universe within the mirror's frame" (1952b, 631). The mirror is only one way to create the double; a woman may also create the double through an inner dialogue, that is, she builds up a figure of herself in her imagination. The narcissist might, for example, cling to childhood memories, recreating the image of herself as a child. She might express her unique personality through her clothes or her "interior"; her mystery is "misunderstood" by those around her.

Beauvoir creates such a character in the short story "Marcelle" in *When Things of the Spirit come First*. As a child, Marcelle thinks of herself as destined to marry greatness. She reads in her aunt's library or reading room. There she sees many adults and dreams they are among the intellectual elite:

> Some of the library's regular visitors aroused a passionate interest in Marcelle: middle-aged men with a pensive gaze, their faces matured and refined by thought. In their handsome greying hair, their overcoats, and their white hands she discerned an exalted elegance that seemed to come from the soul. Perhaps they were writers, poets: they certainly belonged to that intellectual élite that M. Drouffe often spoke about with a mysterious air. Marcelle gazed devoutly upon them. She ardently longed for one of them to notice her some day and to say in velvety tones "What serious books that pretty little girl does read, to be sure!" He would ask her questions and he would be astonished by her replies: then he would take her to a beautiful house

71

full of books and pictures and he would talk to her as though she were grown-up. (Beauvoir 1982, 12)

In *The Second Sex* Beauvoir claims that the narcissist, because of her mystery or "misunderstood treasure," has a need, like the tragic hero, for a ruling destiny. Marcelle sensed her ruling destiny in her youth, "she had the wonderful revelation of her destiny. 'I shall live with a man of genius: I shall be his companion,' she said, in an ecstatic whisper." (1982, 15).

Her delusion continues in her "knowledge" that she is destined to marry greatness and that she, among beings, is unique in her complexity. "In the company of these intellectuals she felt rich with a mysterious femininity, and lonely once again. ... But who would ever be capable of understanding her and loving her weakness? 'The touching weakness of the strong,' she jotted down in a note book; and she promised herself to write a poem ending with those words" (1982, 22). Compare this with what Beauvoir says about the narcissist: "..it is inability to express herself in everyday action that makes the woman believe that she, too, has an inexpressible mystery within her" (1952b, 634).

When she begins spending more time with Denis Charval and his writer friends, she feels she is finally living in the world that was her destiny: "surrounded by young geniuses, she could at last come into bloom" (1982, 29). Again we turn to *The Second Sex* for a fuller explication of the narcissist's bad faith here. Beauvoir offers the following description:

Many women fully convinced of their superiority are incapable, however, of making it manifest to the world; their ambition will then be to use as intermediary some man whom they can impress with their merits. Such a woman does not aim through free projects at values of her own; she wishes to attach ready-made values to her ego, and so she turns to men who possess influence and fame in the hope of identifying herself with them, as inspiration, muse, Egeria" (1952b, 636).

She wishes to steal the transcendence of another because she has subjective desire but no project.

While Denis is gallivanting around town, Marcelle revels in her self-pity. She "sadly remembered the free and peaceful time of her girlhood, when her life ran to the rhythm of melodious verse, when she was surrounded by poets and heroes, brotherly figures always ready to respond to her call, and when she thought about the books she would write in the vague future, about the delicate impressions she had gathered during the day, about happiness, death and fate" (1982, 44).

Denis finally leaves and the tale runs full circle. Marcelle's narcissism is all consuming and she declares the object of her affection:

"All I have is myself," said Marcelle. She closed her eyes: it seemed to her that she was coming back to her real self, as if from a long banishment. Once more she thought of the sad, precocious child, crouching behind heavy curtains that separated her from the world or hiding in the shadows of a book-lined corridor. She saw herself as an adolescent, enthusiastic and misunderstood, confiding her sorrow to a mauve night-sky; she saw her lonely youth, full of pride and high, uncompromising demands. This road, so painfully traversed, had brought her back to solitude; and never again would she be tempted to escape from herself. A great exaltation filled her; she stood up and walked over to the window, drawing the curtains back with a sudden jerk. She was not to look beyond herself for the meaning of her life; she was set free from love, from hope, and from that stifling presence that had taken up all her strength and her time for more than a year. Everything was fine... For the second time she had the wonderful revelation of her fate. "I am a woman of genius," she decided. (1982, 45)

While Marcelle exemplifies one form narcissism may take, there are others worth considering. They are united in their attempt at the impossible unity of the in-itself and the for-itself. Desiring to attain that status is desiring to be God, to eliminate contingency, to flee freedom and responsibility. Yet this is precisely what the narcissist attempts through her self-objectification. As Beauvoir describes her, she is "[a]t once priestess and idol, the narcissist soars haloed with glory through the eternal realm, and below the clouds creatures kneel in adoration; she is God wrapped in self contemplation" (1952b, 632).

The woman from Beauvoir's short story *The Woman Destroyed* is another illustrative example of the effects of narcissism. Beauvoir describes the possible results of narcissism as psychosis — the woman falls away from the actual world in her contemplation of herself as the center of the world. The narcissist who has gone down this road is constantly engaged in self-contemplation but incapable of accurately judging herself. Criticisms from others are understood as jealousy. We see just this sort of narcissistic behavior illustrated in the diary of the woman destroyed. She reinterprets herself and her every action; she mulls over every look and phrase from her husband in a relentless attempt to

73

"understand" her situation. Throughout, she is unaware of the way in which she is lying to herself. "She does not stand on her independence but makes of herself an object that is imperiled by the world and by other conscious beings" (1952b, 640).

The woman in love, like the narcissist, seeks to justify her existence as immanence by embracing it. Beauvoir begins her analysis by noting the differences between the sexes with regard to romantic loving. Whereas men desire possession of a woman while themselves remaining sovereign subjects, for women, "to love is to relinquish everything for the benefit of a master" (1952b, 642). Beauvoir puts this in the terms of her existential ethics:

> The fact is that we have nothing to do here with laws of nature. It is the difference in their situations that is reflected in the difference men and women show in their conceptions of love. The individual who is a subject, who is himself, if he has the courageous inclination toward transcendence, endeavors to extend his grasp on the world: he is ambitious, he acts. But an inessential creature is incapable of sensing the absolute at the heart of her subjectivity; a being doomed to immanence cannot find self-realization in acts. (1952b, 643)

To some extent, we saw that with Marcelle discussed earlier. However, Marcelle was truly in love with herself and used Denis as an instrument for her self-love. The woman in love will forfeit her individuality to be subsumed in that of the man. In some sense, she becomes the ideal feminine-type. She is object for the man's subject; she involves her individual freedom by choosing this object status, that is, she chooses to find her self-realization in her immanence. The woman in love will "try to rise above her situation as inessential object by fully accepting it; through her flesh, her feelings, her behavior, she will enthrone him as supreme value and reality: she will humble herself to nothingness before him" (1952b, 643).

What the woman in love wants is to serve; she must be completely devoted to the man and thereby gain her *raison d'être*. "She at first sought in love a confirmation of what she was, of her past, of her personality; but she also involves her future in it, and to justify her future she puts it in the hands of one who possesses all values. Thus she gives up her transcendence, subordinating it to that of the essential other, to whom she makes herself vassal and slave" (1952b, 651). The woman in love tries to see the world through the eyes of her loved one, she adopts his opinions. The center of the world is not where she is but where her lover is. At one point early in *She Came to Stay*, for example, Françoise describes the world as revolving around her. After Pierre has become infatuated with Xavière, however, she describes the world as revolving around them. She has lost herself because she has become the woman in love. Further evidence of this is her referral to the singularity of their thought prior to the emergence of Xavière on the scene. She and Pierre were "one." Compare this with Beauvoir's later description of the woman in love in *The Second Sex:* "The supreme happiness of the woman in love is to be recognized by the loved man as a part of himself; when he says 'we,' she is associated and identified with him, she shares his prestige and reigns with him over the rest of the world; she never tires of repeating — even to excess — this delectable 'we'" (1952b, 653).

Similarly, in Beauvoir's novel *The Mandarins* we see an example of the woman in love. Paule abdicates herself and her independence to be Henri's mistress. When he stops loving her, she turns to self-loathing. The move from "generous warmth" to masochism is an easy one; if the woman thinks her lover loves her less than she wants or that she fails to satisfy him, she resorts to self-disgust.

"The supreme goal of human love, as of mystical love, is identification with the loved one" (1952b, 653). The woman in love seeks to live her transcendence vicariously through her lover. Sleep, according to Beauvoir, becomes her enemy for it is when her lover is sleeping that she recognizes the immanence of his person: "But the god, the master, should not give himself up to the repose of immanence; the woman views this blasted transcendence with a hostile eye; she detests the animal inertia of this body which exists no longer *for her* but *in itself"* (1952b, 657).

Like the narcissist who creates the very downfall of her own attempts at freedom within immanence, the woman in love sometimes ends up denying the liberty of her lover so that he may remain her master; she disapproves of his ventures and judges him; "she is a jailer" (1952b, 658), that is, she creates the conditions for her failure at loving within immanence. Real love requires subjective reciprocity. The woman in love abdicates her subjectivity in favor of the feminine objectivity she perceives as desired by her lover. In actuality, her lover desires a free being. Paradoxically, while woman imprisons her lover, she also demands his transcendence; she gives him her transcendence and he must act on the world. Woman desires to possess man but a free being cannot be possessed. The woman in love lives in bad faith: she assumes that the love she offers is matched perfectly while failing to distinguish between love and desire. Such bad faith may result in any number of mental and emotional disturbances ranging from mere jealousy to psychosis.

Whereas the narcissist makes herself the god of her subjective worship, the woman in love makes her lover the god. The mystic turns to directly to God; she makes herself God's servant, embodying the passivity of immanence in the mistaken assumption that such an attitude makes her a receptive instrument for God's will. All three of these justification strategies used by women to embrace their immanence rather than seeking to transcend their situation of Otherness result in self-destructive flights from freedom. If each of these is instead integrated with a "life of activity and independence" then it might be possible for the individual to live authentically. By themselves, however, they demonstrate the woman's attempt to "create an unreal relation" lacking "any grasp on the world" (1952b, 678).

The Second Sex is ultimately an optimistic assessment of woman's potential as liberated human being. With regard to human love, woman's potential is realized only when she loves freely without renunciation of her transcendence. "On the day when it will be possible for woman to love not in her weakness but in her strength, not to escape herself but to find herself, not to abase herself but to assert herself — on that day love will become for her, as for man, a source of life and not a mortal danger" (1952b, 669).

The Liberated Life

Although she is often criticized for not offering more of a concrete proposal for woman's liberation, Beauvoir does discuss various changes that need to be made in order for woman to be free. The important thing to note in this regard is that no one area of woman's life constitutes the most damaging or limiting aspect of her oppressed condition; all aspects of woman's situation need to be transformed. This section briefly presents some of the major obstacles that need to be overcome and some of the hopes that Beauvoir articulates as she envisions the life of the independent woman.

Earlier, in the discussion of ethics, we saw that Beauvoir is foremost among the existentialists for arguing for a conception of subjective reciprocity. This reciprocity entails the mutual recognition of the other's freely chosen project. Each individual is both transcendence and immanence; reciprocity requires that we assert our own transcendence while we simultaneously acknowledge the transcendence of the other. Neither individual becomes object for the other's subject. Beauvoir offers reciprocity as a model for genuine love in response to the corrupt love of the justifications. As she argues,

Genuine love ought to be founded on the mutual recognition of two liberties; the lovers would then experience themselves both as self and as other: neither would give up transcendence, neither would be mutilated; together they would manifest values and aims in the world. For the one and the other, love would be revelation of self by the gift of self and enrichment of the world (1952b, 667).

For woman to attain "genuine love" or "reciprocity" she needs herself to be an authentic individual, engaged in projects employing her liberty in human society. She must, in other words, be "The Independent Woman." Beauvoir's solution to woman's situation is complex and controversial. She lauded the ideals of socialism as the necessary conditions for woman's liberated existence. Women, she claimed, need economic freedom along with civil liberties. It is through work, being active and productive, that woman regains her transcendence. But work alone does not ensure a non-oppressed existence. Working conditions must be fair. Socialism is needed so that when women go to work they will not be exploited like workers under capitalism are. Socialism would allow us to create a world wherein women are not required to do both the work of the home and the workplace. It would ensure fair wages for both men and women rather than continue the practice of underpaying women based on the expectation that they will marry. But just working conditions are insufficient for full liberation for woman. Because she has had a different upbringing, and because she has a different perspective, she will not be seen as identical to man. Nonetheless, there are some women who find economic and social autonomy in their work, facilitating political and social responsibility.

Although man's subjectivity and flesh are not at odds, for the independent woman, they are; the independent woman is expected to repudiate her physical side but, Beauvoir argues, as a human being she is also sexual. The independent woman knows she will be judged by her appearance and yet women's clothing is not designed for an active life of independence. A woman feels the pull of femininity and the desire to appear well-dressed but often the fashions defeat her aim of free activity and/or inhibit her ability to be perceived as a transcendent being. Women may also feel the pull to remain feminine with regard to household chores according to Beauvoir. The independent woman has a tendency to respond by doubling her work load. She manages the tasks of her career as well as those of her home. Both of these tensions have been widely addressed by contemporary feminists. Women's fashion magazines are often accused of contributing to the unhealthy relationships many women have to their bodies that may be manifest in eating disorders. With regard to the work problem, liberal feminists have waged an intense battle to change the face of the work environment while simultaneously working to change the distribution of labor within the home. By encouraging more men to take responsibilities within the home and by encouraging employers to experiment with flexible work schedules, women are beginning to see a real change in their work load.

Next, Beauvoir argues that in order to be fully emancipated, woman also needs "access to the other." This is a call that radical feminists have taken up in varying forms. Challenging the gender roles of who is responsible for initiating sexual activity furthers the challenge of gender roles in other social relations as well. Men as well as women must adjust to the sexual and social equality of women. "If [men] would be willing to love an equal instead of a slave — as, it must be added, do those among them who are at once free from arrogance and without an inferiority complex — women would not be as haunted as they are by concern for their femininity..." (1952b, 686). But with this sexual freedom comes great risk, not the least of which are health and safety. Woman also runs the risk of compromising her reputation or career in attempting to satisfy her sexual desires. Liberating women sexually requires confronting some of the paradoxes of their situation. For instance, femininity tells woman to be passive but this may not satisfy her. Independence tells woman to be dominant, but this may also cause sexual problems. Beauvoir postulates that there must be an equal reciprocation, mutual recognition in equality, for there to be equality and satisfaction in sexual relationships. She further argues, however, that it is more difficult for the woman to regard her partner as equal than it is for the man. The woman knows that the man has freely made himself and thus his mistakes are less acceptable. Finally, the independent woman's desires lead her toward monogamy and yet the trappings of domestic life may enslave her.

The independent woman is at something of an impasse when it comes to maternity. She must rely on an other: "There is one feminine function that it is actually almost impossible to perform in complete liberty. It is maternity" (1952b, 696). But pregnancy and motherhood need not be paralyzing activities. Beauvoir believes that freedom of maternity, the freedom to chose whether or not to have a child regardless of one's marital status and when to have a child, will be fully accepted by society. The signs that will indicate social acceptance of freely chosen maternity are safe and legal abortion, affordable contraception, availability of artificial insemination, social support of parenthood, and acceptance of working women with children. As we saw also in the section on motherhood above, work can actually help ease physiological pain of childbearing because it helps to take the woman's mind off of it, it gives her something else to be concerned with and demonstrates that her life is not confined to the perpetuation of the species.

In terms of intellectual pursuits, the independent woman must overcome the obstacles put in place by society. Perhaps the most challenging of these obstacles is the woman's inferiority complex. When Beauvoir wrote *The Second Sex*, women had to attain acceptance into the realms of society formerly occupied only by men. Even while still a student, a girl may find her creativity and inventiveness lost. Girls may be reluctant to participate in intellectual pursuits for fear of being regarded as "bluestockings" or overly intellectual. Women must constantly win the confidence of others and gain the respect of others with whom they work. The hope is that woman will cast off her feelings of inferiority while society discards its perception of women as socially and intellectually limited to traditionally feminine fields.

With this hope in mind, Beauvoir adds that there are some careers that blend transcendence and the social prescriptions of femininity. Actresses, dancers, singers, for example, have careers that in fact enhance their femininity. Indeed, Beauvoir cites their historical independence in society. Such women have enjoyed a greater degree of freedom because they embody the social expectations of femininity while also pursuing their own projects. Recall, however, that Beauvoir distinguishes artists from the movie harlots. The latter attempt to justify their position of immanence rather than pursue transcendence.

Literature and art are also activities women turn to for salvation. However, due to lack of training, women's artistic expression often reflects her situation and results in rather poor literary outcomes. "Women do not contest the human situation, because they have hardly begun to assume it" (1952b, 711).

Woman's situation inclines her to seek salvation in literature and art. Living marginally to the masculine world, she sees it not in its universal form but from her special point of view. For her it is no conglomeration of implements and concepts, but a source of sensations and emotions; her interest in the qualities of things is drawn by the gratuitous and hidden elements in them. Taking an attitude of negation and denial, she is not absorbed in the real; she protests against it, with words. She seeks through nature for the image of her soul, she abandons herself to reveries, she wishes to attain her *being*--but she is doomed to frustration; she can recover it only in the region of the imaginary. To prevent an inner life that has no *useful* purpose from sinking into nothingness, to assert herself against given conditions which she bears rebelliously, to create a

79

world other than that in which she fails to attain her being, she must resort to *self-expression* (Beauvoir 1952b, 662-663).

A great writer, according to Beauvoir, is to be a part of the world and yet distanced from it: "In order to create...it is necessary to want to reveal the world to others; consequently, one must be able to see the world, and in order to do so one must attain a certain distance from it. When totally immersed in a situation, you cannot describe it" (Beauvoir 1987, 27). The good writer knows her words form interpersonal communication with the reader; the bad writer assumes words express her own feelings. But in order to be successful, any artistic endeavor must be undertaken in freedom. "Art, literature, philosophy, are attempts to found the world anew on a human liberty: that of the individual creator; to entertain such a pretension, one must first unequivocally assume the status of a being who has liberty....what woman needs first of all is to undertake, in anguish and pride, her apprenticeship in abandonment and transcendence: that is, in liberty" (1952b, 711). Similarly, Beauvoir praises the literature of protest, that is, women writers who have challenged an unjust society.

> And that is why I said that women are well placed to describe the society, the world, the time to which they belong, but only to a certain extent. Truly great works are those which contest the world in its entirety. Now that is something which women just do not do. They will criticize, they will challenge certain details; but as for contesting the world in its entirety — to do that it is necessary to feel deeply responsible for the world. (Beauvoir 1987, 28)

With literature, as with any project, the existent must break free of the restraints. Women must confront their status as the Other and men must give up their delusion of being the Absolute.

Since *The Second Sex*

The Second Sex is Beauvoir's most important legacy. She began the conversation about women that provided generations of women valuable insight into their oppression. Feminists all over the world have taken up the challenges posed by *The Second Sex.* Yet it was not until the early 1970s that Beauvoir identified herself as a feminist. The very act of writing made her aware of her situation as woman and how she had profited from the male-oriented society. Although she described herself as "not a militant in the strict sense" (Schwarzer 1984, 69), Beauvoir certainly was actively involved in feminist campaigns. Talking with Alice Schwarzer in 1976, Beauvoir identified abortion and contraception, domestic violence, language, work, and motherhood and marriage as the women's issues that most concerned her. Violence against women was the most prominent recurring theme in the interviews Beauvoir conducted during the last two decades of her life. She also deepened her analysis to emphasize the interconnection of different forms of oppression. In an interview with John Gerassi, Beauvoir argues that "embodied in [woman's] revolt for sexual equality is the demand for class equality" (Gerassi 1976, 81). In addition, she makes several analogies between racial oppression and sexist oppression.

Gerassi also asked about a follow-up to *The Second Sex*. Rejecting the notion that she write another book on women, Beauvoir did propose an interesting alternative. Beauvoir suggested that women from all over the world and of varying social classes write about their lived experience. The stories could be collected and analyzed for similarities. More importantly, such a collection would challenge feminist theory to expand beyond the interests of middle-class intellectuals and "derive our theory from practice, not the other way around" (Gerassi 1976, 84).

6
Liberation

The Second Sex ends with Beauvoir's illustration of the independent woman. Although this proposal has met with ample criticism, it nonetheless serves as a stepping stone for comprehending liberation not just for women but for all oppressed groups. One important thing the "independent woman" shows us is that liberation must not be solely an individual struggle. Social transformation is required together with the transformation of the individual. Indeed, after the writing of *The Second Sex* Beauvoir herself became much more political. This chapter focuses on Beauvoir's struggle to bring about social change in her philosophy and her practical involvement.

During the 1950s and 60s Beauvoir undertook the writing of her memoirs. This colossal project resulted in a four volume autobiography that details her thoughts, intellectual disputes, political involvement, friendships and daily trials and tribulations. While the first volume chronicles her youth, the final three volumes detail her adult activity. Careful reading of her autobiography reveals a Beauvoir who was virtually unaware of political events until her own life was profoundly affected by them. World War II marks the most dramatic turning point but Beauvoir was also awakened from her self-absorption by the turmoil of Stalin's communism, the racial situation in the United States, the crisis in Algeria, and the events of May 1968.

During the Algerian crisis, Beauvoir used her notoriety to protest the French torture of Algerians and united with lawyer Gisele Halimi to publish a book on the torture of Djamila Boupacha, a young Algerian woman. On June 3rd, 1960, an article by Beauvoir appeared in *Le Monde* detailing the torture of Boupacha by personnel under French control.

More to the point, Beauvoir tried to sway public opinion and arouse public responsibility. The article begins by noting the desensitizing effects of scandalous behavior, that is, that the public remains indifferent in the face of a tragic scandal precisely because such scandal has become commonplace. This chilling social reprimand is followed up at the end of the article with a call for social responsibility:

...an abdication of responsibility would be a betrayal of France as a whole, of you, of me, of each and every one of us. For whether we choose our rulers willingly, or submit to them against our natural inclinations, we remain their accomplices whether we like it or not. When the government of a country allows crimes to be committed in its name, every citizen thereby becomes a member of a collectively criminal nation. (Beauvoir and Halimi 1962, 197)

This experience, like the call for social transformation on behalf of gender equality, indicates Beauvoir's commitment to solidarity. As we saw in the chapter on Beauvoir's ethics, solidarity with others is presumed in an individual's freedom. "And it is true that each is bound to all; but that is precisely the ambiguity of his condition: in his surpassing toward others, each one exists absolutely as for himself; each is interested in the liberation of all, but as a separate existence engaged in his own projects" (1948, 112). Beauvoir's solidarity ethics arises from the unlikely sources of an existentialism founded on the individual and yet, as she has argued, that individualism is precisely its strength. If each existent is recognized as unique then the unity of all would be a unity of each to every other. The result is that each individual is irreplaceable to the whole (1948, 108). Her novel, *The Blood of Others* (1945) is a literary exploration of this theme. Indeed, the epigraph of that novel is from Dostoevski: "Each of us is responsible for everything and to every human being."

In addition to solidarity, Beauvoir lauded the potential of socialism. The economic equality promised under socialism is the means, Beauvoir argues, by which woman will gain her social equality. Proper socialism would not relegate woman to the domestic sphere but instead would oblige her to participate in the production of the society. Socialism would also not abandon her to being the sole care-giver of children. The following from *The Second Sex* illustrates the promise of socialism, though Beauvoir also recognizes that the promise remains unfulfilled:

A world where men and women would be equal is easy to visualize, for that precisely is what the Soviet Revolution *promised*: women raised and trained exactly like men were to work under the same conditions and for the same wages. Erotic liberty was to be recognized by custom, but the sexual act was not to be considered a "service" to be paid for; woman was to be *obliged* to provide herself with other ways of earning a living; marriage was to be based on a free agreement that the spouses could break at will; maternity was to be voluntary, which meant that contraception and abortion were to be authorized and that, on the other hand, all mothers and their children were to have exactly the same rights, in or out of marriage; pregnancy leaves were to be paid for by the State, which would assume charge of the children, signifying not that they would be *taken away* from their parents, but that they would not be *abandoned* to them. (1952b, 724-725; see also 525)

Notice how this quotation responds to many of the aspects of woman's oppressive situation discussed in *The Second Sex*. Beauvoir has detailed the freedom limiting aspects of woman's situation and her proposal for overcoming them is, in large part, socialism. In her later years she realized that socialism alone was not enough, that woman's oppression extended far deeper than could be addressed solely through economic transformation (Schwarzer 1972; Gerassi 1976, 80). It is also worth noting that her novel, *The Mandarins* (1960) reveals the disappointment with communism as it illustrates the dilemma of the left in the face of Stalin's death camps. Communism, too, had become oppressive.

A final element to Beauvoir's thoughts on liberation pertains to the aesthetic. Beauvoir praises the literature of protest, for example, women writers who have challenged an unjust society. While literature is her favored medium of social criticism, art and philosophy also "attempt to found the world anew on a human liberty." As such, they require the individual to "assume the status of a being who has liberty" and creatively act on the world in transcendence (1952b, 711). Literature is privileged in this task of liberation or salvation because it allows the writer to communicate with the reader, disclosing the world without statically defining it. The reader interprets through his or her own experience what the writer has revealed of his or her experience. For the writer, the purpose of literature is "to make manifest the equivocal, separate, contradictory truths that no one moment represents in their totality, either inside or outside myself" (1964, 263; see also Beauvoir 1965).

Women and other oppressed groups are ideally situated to fulfill the liberatory function of literature. Their status as Other means they have a sort of privileged perspective from which to critique society (Beauvoir 1987). Cultural expression, in the form of art, literature, and philosophy, dismantles the oppressive structures from the inside. The "revolt" is carried on through the myth-making aspects of culture. This proposal for liberation seems somewhat paradoxical however. The individual is asked to act in liberty in order to transform his or her oppressive situation. Yet the oppressive situation keeps the individual from exercising his or her liberty to its fullest potential. The paradox is resolved in that Beauvoir's proposal is dialectic. The individual acts and culture is transformed, the culture is transformed thereby allowing the individual to expand his or her creative abilities.

> ...man is at once the end and the means of economic and social changes, while culture is man himself as he speaks of himself and of the world that is his; while expressing the state of humanity, culture must contribute to the bettering of man's fate; the technological revolution still being short of completion, culture is today, the instrument to a progress of which it will tomorrow be the consummation. (1959, 228)

Even speaking from a situation of oppression, the existent has the power to transform the universal via the articulation of particular experience. The first step in the dialectic is to renounce resignation to one's situation and recognize one's obligation to disclose the world. "Truly great works are those which contest the world in its entirety....to do that it is necessary to feel deeply responsible for the world" (Beauvoir 1987, 28).

On the whole, Beauvoir's philosophy is a full of optimism. Her own personal desire for happiness, her belief in the potential of human freedom, and her recognition of the possibilities of gender equality infuse existentialism with new vigor as well as new responsibility. Philosophy and philosophers must not be content to contemplate the world. The philosophy of lived experience asks us also to remain ever vigilant in our social criticism, politics, and liberation struggles.

Bibliography

Ascher, Carol. 1981. *Simone de Beauvoir: A Life of Freedom.* Boston: Beacon Press.
Bair, Deirdre. 1986. Simone de Beauvoir: Politics, Language, and Feminist Identity. *Yale French Studies.* 72:149-164.
-----. 1990. *Simone de Beauvoir: A Biography.* New York: Summit Books.
Beauvoir, Simone de. 1944. *Pyrrhus et Cinéas.* Paris: Gallimard.
-----. 1947. Eye for Eye. Translated by Mary McCarthy. *Politics.* (July-August): 134-140.
-----. 1948. *The Ethics of Ambiguity.* Translated by Bernard Frechtman. Secaucus, NJ: Citadel Press.
-----. 1952a. *America Day by Day.* Translated by Patrick Dudley. London: G. Duckworth.
-----. 1952b. *The Second Sex.* Translated by H. M. Parshley. New York: Bantam Books. Reprinted 1989. New York: Vintage Books.
-----. 1954. *She Came to Stay.* New York: W.W. Norton & Company.
-----. 1955. *Priviléges.* Paris: Gallimard.
-----. 1958. *The Long March.* Translated by Austryn Wainhouse. New York: World Publishing Company.
-----. 1959. *Memoirs of a Dutiful Daughter.* Translated by James Kirkup. Cleveland: World.
-----. 1960. *The Mandarins.* Translated by Leonard M. Friedman. New York: Meridian Books.
-----. 1962a. Must we Burn Sade? In *The Marquis de Sade* edited by Paul Dinage. London: John Calder.
-----. 1962b. *Prime of Life.* Translated by Peter Green. New York: The World Publishing Company.
-----. 1964a. *Force of Circumstances.* Translated by Richard Howard. New York: G.P. Putnam's Sons.
-----. 1964b. Introduction to Perrault's Tales. New York: MacMillian Company.
-----. 1965a. Que Peut la Littérature? In *Que Peut La Littérature?* Edited by Yves Buin. Union Générale d'Éditions. (Author's Translation).

Bibliography

-----. 1965b. *A Very Easy Death*. Translated by Patrick O'Brian. New York: Random House. [1964 Gallimard].

-----. 1965c. What Love Is — and Isn't. *McCall's*. (August): 71, 133.

-----. 1968. *Les Belle Images*. New York: Putnam. [1966 Gallimard]

-----. 1969. *The Woman Destroyed*. Translated by Patrick O'Brian. New York: Pantheon Books. [1968 Gallimard]

-----. 1972a. *Brigitte Bardot and the Lolita Syndrome*. New York: Reynal and Company. [1959 *Esquire*]

-----. 1972b. *Coming of Age*. Translated by Patrick O'Brian. New York: G.P. Putnam's Sons.

-----. 1974a. *All Said and Done*. Translated by Patrick O'Brian. New York: Putnam's.

-----. 1974b. *The Blood of Others*. Translated by Roger Senhouse and Yvonne Moyse. New York: Bantam Books 1974 [1945 Gallimard].

-----. 1974c. "Les Femmes s'entetent." *Les Temps Modernes*. (April-May).

-----. 1982. *When Things of the Spirit Come First*. Translated by Patrick O'Brian. New York: Pantheon Books.

-----. 1983 *Who Shall Die? (Les Bouches Inutiles)*. Translated by Claude Francis and Fernande Gontier. Florissant, MO: River Press.

-----. 1985. *Adieux: A Farewell to Sartre*. Translated by Patrick O'Brian. Harmondsworth: Penguin.

-----. 1987. Women and Creativity. In *French Feminist Thought: A Reader*, edited by Toril Moi. New York: Basil Blackwell.

-----. 1991. *Letters to Sartre*. Translated and edited by Quintin Hoare. New York: Arcade. [1990 Gallimard].

-----. 1992. *All Men are Mortal*. Translated by Leonard M. Friedman. New York: W.W. Norton and Co. [1946 Gallimard].

-----. 1998. *A Transatlantic Love Affair: Letters to Nelson Algren*. New York: The New Press.

Beauvoir, Simone de and Gisele Halimi. 1962. *Djamila Boupacha*. Translated by Peter Green. New York: MacMillan Company. [1962 Gallimard].

Bell, Linda. 1993. *Rethinking Ethics in the Midst of Violence*. Lanham, MD: Rowman and Littlefield.

Bergoffen, Debra B. 1997. *The Philosophy of Simone de Beauvoir: Gendered Phenomenologies, Erotic Generosities*. Albany, NY: SUNY Press.

Brosman, Catharine Savage. 1991. *Simone de Beauvoir Revisited*. Boston: Twayne Publishers.

Dallery, Arleen B. 1990. Sexual Embodiment: Beauvoir and French Feminism (*ecriture feminine*). In Al-Hibri, Azizah and Margaret Simons, eds., *Hypatia Reborn*. Indiana University Press, Indianapolis, IN.

Dietz, Mary G. 1992. Debating Simone de Beauvoir. *Signs* 18(1): 74-88.

Evans, Mary. 1985. *Simone de Beauvoir: A Feminist Mandarin*. London: Tavistock.

Fallaize, Elizabeth. 1990. *The Novels of Simone de Beauvoir*. New York: Routledge Press.

Fichera, Virginia. 1986. Simone de Beauvoir and 'The Woman Question': *Les Bouches Inutiles*. *Yale French Studies* 72: 51-66.

Francis, Claude and Fernande Gontier. 1987. *Simone de Beauvoir: A Life...A Love Story.* Translated by Lisa Nesselson. New York: St. Martins Press.

Fraser, Nancy. 1992. Introduction. In *Revaluing French Feminism: Critical Essays on Difference, Agency, and Culture,* edited by Nancy Fraser and Sandra Lee Bartky. Bloomington: Indiana University Press.

Friedan, Betty. 1976. Interview with Simone de Beauvoir. In *It Changed my Life.* New York: Random House.

Fullbrook, Kate and Edward Fullbrook. 1994. *Simone de Beauvoir and Jean-Paul Sartre: The Remaking of a Twentieth-Century Legend.* New York: Basic Books.

-----. 1998. *Simone de Beauvoir: A Critical Introduction.* Malden, MA: Blackwell Publishers.

Gerassi, John. 1976. Simone de Beauvoir: *The Second Sex:* 25 Years Later. *Society* (January/February): 79-85.

Hatcher, Donald L. 1989. Existential Ethics and Why it's Immoral to be a Housewife. *The Journal of Value Inquiry* 23: 59-68.

Jardine, Alice. 1979. Interview with Simone de Beauvoir. *Signs: Journal of Women in Culture and Society* 5(2):229-230.

John, Helen James, S.N.D. 1976. The Promise of Freedom in the Thought of Simone de Beauvoir: "How an Infant Smiles." *Proceedings of the American Catholic Phil. Assoc.* V. 50. Edited by George McLean. Washington: Office of the National Secretary of the Assoc., Catholic Univ. of America.

Kruks, Sonia. 1992. Gender and Subjectivity: Simone de Beauvoir and Contemporary Feminism. *Signs: Journal of Women in Culture and Society* 18(1): 89-110.

-----. 1995. Simone de Beauvoir: Teaching Sartre about freedom. In *Feminist Interpretations of Simone de Beauvoir,* edited by Margaret Simon. University Park, PA: Penn State University Press.

Kuykendall, Eleanor H. 1989. Simone de Beauvoir and Two Kinds of Ambivalence in Action. In *The Thinking Muse.* Edited by Jeffner Allen and Iris Marion Young. Bloomington: Indiana University Press.

Lamblin, Bianca. *A Disgraceful Affair.* Translated by Julie Plovnick. Boston: Northeastern University Press, 1996.

Langer, Monika. 1994. A Philosophical Retrieval of Simone de Beauvoir's *Pour une Morale de L'Ambiguité. Philosophy Today* (Summer): 181-190.

Lundgren-Gothlin, Eva. 1994. Simone de Beauvoir and Ethics. *History of European Ideas* 19(4-5): 899-903.

-----. 1996. *Sex and Existence: Simone de Beauvoir's The Second Sex.* London: Athlone Press.

Lydon, Mary. 1987. Hats and cocktails: Simone de Beauvoir's Heady Texts. In *Critical Essays on Simone de Beauvoir,* edited by Elaine Marks. Boston: G.K. Hall & Company.

Marks, Elaine. 1973. *Simone de Beauvoir: Encounters with Death.* New Brunswick, NJ: Rutgers University Press.

-----. 1978. Women and Literature in France. *Signs: Journal of Women in Culture and Society* 3(4): 832-842.

McBride, William. 1995. Philosophy, Literature, and Everyday Life in Beauvoir and Sartre. Paper presented at the Sartre Society-Beauvoir Circle Meeting, SPEP, 12 October, Chicago, Illinois.

Merleau-Ponty, Maurice. 1964. Metaphysics and the Novel. In *Sense and Non-sense*. Translated by Hubert Dreyfus and Patricia Allen Dreyfus. Chicago: Northwestern University Press.

Moi, Toril. 1990. *Feminist Theory and Simone de Beauvoir*. Cambridge, MA: Basil Blackwell.

-----. 1994. *Simone de Beauvoir: The Making of an Intellectual Woman*. Cambridge, MA: Blackwell Publishers.

Morgan, Kathryn Pauly. 1986. Romantic Love, Altruism, and Self-Respect: An Analysis of Simone de Beauvoir. *Hypatia* 1(1): 117-148.

Murphy, Julien. 1995. Beauvoir and the Algerian War: Toward a Post-colonial Ethics. In *Feminist Interpretations of Simone de Beauvoir*, edited by Margaret Simons. University Park, PA: Pennsylvania State University Press.

Okely, Judith. 1986. *Simone de Beauvoir*. London: Virago.

Pilardi, Jo-Ann. 1991. Philosophy Becomes autobiography. In *Writing the Politics of Difference*, ed. by Hugh Silverman. Albany, NY: SUNY Press.

Sartre, Jean-Paul. 1953. *Being and Nothingness*. Translated by Hazel E. Barnes. New York: Philosophical Library. [1943 Gallimard].

-----. 1988. *What is Literature? and Other Essays*. Translated by Steven Ungar. Cambridge, MA: Harvard University Press.

Schwarzer, Alice. 1972. Interview with Simone de Beauvoir. *Ms.* (July).

-----. 1984. *After the Second Sex*. Translated by Marianne Howarth. New York: Pantheon Books.

Singer, Linda. 1985. Interpretation and retrieval: rereading Beauvoir. *Hypatia (WSIF)* 3: 231-238.

Simons, Margaret. 1989. Two Interviews with Simone de Beauvoir. *Hypatia* 3(3):11-27.

-----. 1992. Lesbian Connections. *Signs* 18(1): 136-161.

-----. 1995. *Feminist Interpretations of Simone de Beauvoir*. University Park: Pennsylvania State University Press.

-----. 1999. *Beauvoir and the Second Sex*. New York: Rowman and Littlefield.

Vintges, Karen. 1996. *Philosophy as Passion: The Thinking of Simone de Beauvoir*. Bloomington, IN: Indiana University Press.

Zerilli, Linda M. G. 1992. A Process without a Subject: Simone de Beauvoir and Julia Kristeva on Maternity. *Signs* 18(1): 111-135.